School Bus Sass

Amazing Encounters
with My Kids

THERESE MILETI

School Bus Sass

Amazing Encounters with My Kids

This book is a collection of real-life events. However, some of the names, places, and other incidents may have been changed to protect the identity of those individuals involved from any liability, embarrassment, or any type of identification for their personal protection.

Edited, formatted, and cover created by
Author's Bridge Publishing
A CyberDiamond, LLC Company
320 Mamie Cook Road
Boone, NC 28607-7844

ISBN-13: 978-0-692-59354-7
ISBN-10: 0-692-59354-3

Cover photo shot by Ken Logan
About Author photo by Dominic Mileti
Author's website: www.schoolbusdiary.com

School Bus Sass

Amazing Encounters
with My Kids

THERESE MILETI

CONTENTS

DEDICATION ix

PROLOGUE 1

Once in a Blue Moon... 14

Truth Be Told 17

Post it.. 21

Super Sticky Situation...................................... 25

Bubble Gum Mayhem....................................... 28

The Wheels of Change...................................... 32

I Know a Shortcut.. 34

Kinder-garbage... 39

Peek-a-boo 43

Zoo Crew 47

I Do 51

Dance Fever 55

Lip Smackers 57

Manic Monday... 59

Bully Bully 68

You're Never Fully Dressed Without a Smile
70

Where There's Smoke.... 72

Bonjour 76

It's Just a Number 78

Internet Sensation 80

First Day Excitement 84

Five Good Reasons 86

Filter This... 89

Just a Little Kiss 92

Mother May I 96

Easy Reader 99

Just a Little Wiggle..102

Cupcake Anyone?...105

Monday Monday...108

Super-Size Me...110

Mirror Mirror 113

Auto Response 116

B-L-E-E-P...118

One is Such a Lonely Number 122

Just a Little Crush..123

Flash Dance 125

45 Billion Years Ago.......................................127

Bieber Fever 132

I Have a Question 134

Unforgettable 138

Hocus Pocus..143

Reserved Seating 150

Dirty Dancing 153

Sassy Pants.. 155

Check...1...2...Check............................... 157

Fun Start to My Day 159

Nothing to Talk About............................. 161

Once Bitten.. 163

Can I Have This Dance? 165

Joy to the World? 167

Remote Control 169

Gotta Go.. 170

Not Quite Ready 172

Karate Kid.. 174

Looking Good 175

Only the Lonely....................................... 176

Kidisms 177

My Children.. 185

About the Author 186

Acknowledgements 188

DEDICATION

For my kids.

PROLOGUE

When I started driving a school bus, I had no idea how profoundly this job would impact my life, the joy I would find, and all of the amazing people I would meet. I have always shared stories about the children I transport and the daily adventures we have together. I had never considered writing them down, nor had I tried to compile them into a book for others to enjoy. The idea really was not my own and I have a number of family members, friends, and coworkers whose encouragement made this all possible, and for which I am truly grateful. Thank you for continually encouraging me to keep on keeping on!

It is my hope that anyone reading this book will find themselves smiling, be filled with joy, and maybe even occasionally laugh aloud. There may even be a tear or two in there as well.

To all my fellow school bus drivers, I encourage you to jot down your stories. Tell them to your friends and families, for they will be the memories you hold near and dear to your heart, even when you are no longer transporting America's children, our children.

Before I share with you how the wheels on the bus go round and round, it might be helpful to know when and why the wheels started turning.

I started the process of getting my C.D.L. (Commercial Driver's License) back in February 2001. My husband and I made the parenting choice of having one of us remain at home after we had our child in May of 1995, as luck would have it, that honor was bestowed upon me. When Dominic turned five, however, I knew I wanted to go back to work, at least part-time anyway. There was a problem, I only wanted to work while my child was in school, which meant that I would need nights, weekends, and holidays...oh and did I mention that I even wanted the entire summer off as well. Where was I going to find a job that had a schedule that would meet my needs with a desirable salary to accompany it? Yeah right!

My background was in retail management and we all know there is not a retail job around that would accommodate the very time specific work schedule I was interested in obtaining. Having been in retail and conducting the interviewing process routinely, I knew exactly the type of response I would have received from a potential employer. Anyone who has ever worked retail will know exactly where I am coming from.

Let me get this straight, you want to work Monday through Friday from 10:00 AM till 2:00 PM,

2

you cannot work nights, weekends, or any holidays, and you want to be off for 10-weeks during the summer? I am certain any potential interviewers' reactions would have ranged from sheer amusement to complete irritation by me wasting their time. Therefore, to avoid that scenario, I searched for alternate employment opportunities.

I briefly considered going back to school to attain teaching credentials, but quickly discounted that idea. The time and effort it would take to achieve that goal seemed like such a daunting task and one that I was not prepared to undertake. So my search continued.

I set my sights on secretarial work and in particular secretarial work within the school district. Frankly, I would have been a miserable secretary. My software knowledge of Excel and some other commonly used software programs are shall we say—well, they are less than stellar! It was not long before I changed directions once again.

Searching through the local paper, and by local, I mean small town paper that is printed only weekly. I think every small town across America has their very own version of these journalistic gems. As I skipped over the really important information like engagements, weddings, births, and obituaries, which typically are the highlights of this type of paper, I moved on to what really mattered—garage sale postings. Oops, sidetracked again. I managed to make my way to the jobs section of the want ads and while searching the many rows of truck drivers, nurses, and restaurant opportunities available, I knew none of them would allow for my very inflexible schedule. Then, while perusing the ads under the driver's section, there was an ad for school bus drivers for the city we were living in at that time. I pointed the ad out to my husband and we both laughed at the prospect of me becoming a school bus driver. I closed the paper, leaving my quest for employment for another day. Two weeks passed and I was once again searching through the local want ads. Not much had changed as far as what was listed, including the same ad for school bus drivers. This time, however, I called the number listed in the paper and spoke with the transportation supervisor, Nancy Belle Gordon. Nancy told me all about her experience as a school bus driver and how working as a school bus driver still afforded her the opportunity to continue raising her seven children in the process. She shared with me about how flexible the schedule was and how she was able to manage her family life with the ability to bring her children to work with her. She was hitting all of schedule requirements and the pay was good. Then, Nancy caught me off guard by stating there was a class starting the next day that I should attend, and start the process of becoming a bona fide school bus driver. As a result of our conversation my journey to becoming a school bus driver began. I do not think I could have shocked my husband more when I called him at work to inform him that I would start training to become a school bus driver the next day!

Of course, my husband had some concerns for my well-being; you see I am not a particularly tall or large person. The reality is I am five foot nothing and... well, you get the point, I am down right small. So, the what-ifs were going through his mind. The potentially scary what-ifs like—a large high school person wanting to inflict harm upon me, or the middle school, or the elementary person; OK, well maybe not the elementary school person. I must tell you to date, my one and only death threat has come from a second grader. Yes, you read that correctly, a second grader...more on that later! Then, there were the silly and absurd what ifs, like what if your feet will not reach the accelerator pedal? HA HA! Very funny! My response was "Really, Nick?" Besides, they must have pedal extenders, right?

I was given the phone number of another hopeful Aurora school bus driver, Melody. Together, along with a classroom full of school bus driver wannabe's, we started our pre-service classes. Our instructors name was Kent Barker. One of the very first things out of his mouth was "If you think you're gonna get rich as a school bus driver, I'm here to tell you that's never gonna happen, so you might want to leave now." Hmmm, I am not sure if Kent was expecting it, but three people immediately got up out of their seats and walked right out the door. Any other brilliant news flashes you would like to share with the class Kent? Well actually, we lost a few others that week, after we were shown some movies about railroad crossings and about being distracted as a driver. You know, the over the top graphic movies they show you when you are fifteen or sixteen years old and you're taking driver's-ed classes, disturbing images, but effective. We dwindled even further, when we completed the whole liability section of the course. Our class was shrinking and none of us had even stepped foot on a bus yet. Thankfully, the week ended and those of us that remained were eager to start behind the wheel training.

I was being hired for a relatively small school district. There were only about 40 busses in the entire fleet. At the time when I was hired, there was no resident On Board Instructor, or OBI, so one had to be hired out from one of the surrounding communities to complete our onboard instruction. My OBI's name was Twinkle, that is right, Twinkle. Twinkle was not a shortened version of her given name, nor was it a nickname given by friends or family members. That was her actual given name. She was a gem! Fun and funny! However, she did work morning, mid-day, and afternoons making it difficult to schedule time to train with her. Eventually, however, I obtained the required time of behind the wheel needed to schedule my CDL exam.

Twinkle's husband just happened to be a CDL examiner. Can you say convenient?

The day of my exam arrived and I found myself feeling like an awkward 16-year-old preparing to take my first driving test. By the way, was not a particularly fond or favorable memory from my past. I was going to have to relive the nightmarish experience, known as parallel parking, only this time I would be reliving that experience in a 40-foot, 13-ton vehicle. I was beyond nervous! Okay, I must confess, parallel parking a school bus turned out to be a much easier task than parallel parking my parent's car or anyone else's car for that matter. However, parallel parking was not the only trick we were expected to perform while driving a school bus with an examiner onboard. We had to drive a backwards-serpentine formation and as if that was not bad enough they added a loading dock maneuver just for good measure. Wait, a LOADING DOCK maneuver? Really? I mean, I thought I was driving a school bus, not a semi. But yes, a loading dock maneuver. How much fun can one person have? Apparently a lot!

I was schooled on the way to the testing site about a number of mistakes I could make that would bring about an abrupt end to the examination process. These include unsafe maneuvers, such as excessive speed or going too slow, wait—what, one could actually go too slow? The answer to that question is a resounding YES! Believe it or not, you do not impress CDL examiners by going too fast or too slow. She added, hitting curbs, driving with the door open, or without my seatbelt and any traffic violation or accident were the ones that immediately ended the test. It did not include a bunch of minor mistakes that eventually added up to failure. So in other words, no pressure—yeah right!

Did you ever notice that when you are really nervous about something that it goes by in a blur? You know you were present for the event, heck, you even participated in the event, but it feels a bit more like an out of body experience. Well, that is how my CDL practical exam was for me. I passed. I did very well on my pre-trip, surprisingly well on maneuverability, and the road test went just fine. But I do not exactly remember the entire event because most of it went by in a big blur and was over before I knew it. I was the proud recipient of a brand new CDL license with all the endorsements needed to drive a school bus! Then, it hit me. Holy shit—I passed! Now, I would actually have to drive the school bus with kids, lots and lots of kids, and with my back facing them, while I attempted to drive them to and from school safely. What the heck was I thinking?

Typically, when you are hired on as a driver, you start out as a sub-bus driver, a part-time position until a full-time route becomes available. How quickly you obtain a route largely depends on the needs of the district, typically, the wait is about one school year, give or take. Interestingly enough, they actually give the hardest job to the newest, most inexperienced drivers. Only days after receiving a CDL, a sub-driver is given a route sheet. This is exactly what it sounds like, instructions on how to arrive at designated stops to pick up students. They can be taken to the various schools depending on the age group being driven, or delivering them from school to their designated drop off locations. Easier said than done! This can be an especially challenging task when one, such as myself, had recently relocated to the area. And not just from one city to another, or even from one end of the state to the other, but a complete relocation from Memphis, Tennessee to a suburb of Cleveland, Ohio. I know what you are thinking...a proper southern lady blasted into Yankee territory. HA! I am a Minnesota girl born and raised, so I was no stranger to the north or the snow that comes with the territory. Shoot, it was almost like going home when we arrived in Ohio! This did not help me one bit. When I was not acclimated to the area, nor did it help me attain the layout of the city. The point in having said all of that is simple. I had absolutely no idea where I was going! I would soon find out that it was far more challenging than I had ever anticipated.

9

Even after successfully completing my CDL exam, it did not give me the green light to drive with kids onboard. First, I had to meet our pre-service instructors' set of expectations and stamp of approval, prompting another encounter with Kent Barker. There were four of us that day scheduled to get the Kent Barker stamp of approval and since all of us had successfully received our CDL's, we were all kind of expecting this to be a piece of cake, kind of a formality, and pretty much be rubber stamped, get out of jail free type thing. We could not have been more wrong, or further from the truth! He made the state exam look like a walk in the park. Long story short, I was the only one to pass that day. Melody decided she had had enough and her career as a school bus driver came to an abrupt end. Tim and Lee, two other driving hopefuls testing with me that day, made it the second go around. Finally, I was ready to drive the bus WITH kids onboard—or was I?

The first few days, I was put with veteran drivers who were to show me the ropes, so to say, and get me acclimated to the art of driving a fully loaded school bus and follow along with the route sheets provided. Now, back in 2001 computer generated route sheets in the district I started out driving for were shall I say, less than accurate. Many of the drivers prepared their own hand-written route sheets. They were more accurate, and easier to handle while driving than the route sheets provided.

One of the first people I rode with was Al. Al is a terrific person and a good driver. He had a fantastic rapport with his students, though I must say, discipline was not his forte.

As I mentioned earlier, the year was 2001, I was the ripe old age of 34. There is a point to me mentioning this fact and I will get to it in a moment. In this particular district, both middle school and high school students rode the bus simultaneously. You would pick up students at the middle school first; then, drive a short distance to the high school to pick up the high school students. On this particular day, I was riding and observing on Al's bus. We picked up the middle schoolers, and we were waiting at the high school for the students to board. The middle school students were far more observant in noticing that there was a second adult on the bus, in general they both acknowledged my existence and greeted me too. The high school students were, at best, completely oblivious to my presence, somewhat clueless, so to say. Though, in reality they were probably just uninterested. The only interest that most high school students have, in regards to riding a school bus, is to make the misery end as quickly as possible. I mean, could there be anything worse than having to ride a school bus? At that age, it is pretty high on the priority list to be seen on a school bus as little as possible. God forbid, that would mean admitting that you were in one of three undesirable categories, a freshman, an unlicensed sophomore, or gasp—a vehicleless upper classman. Needless to say, my presence was largely undetected. Typically, the oldest kids on the bus occupy the back of the bus. It is true at most age levels. Therefore, in this instance, the high school students were in the back and the middle schoolers, any place a high school student was not.

When you are picking up two groups of students at the same time, it makes for a very crowded bus. The capacity of the bus we were in that day was 78. Realize this folks that means putting three nearly adult-sized people per seat with their backpacks and all the other stuff they might be carrying with them, i.e. musical instruments, school projects, etc. Sometimes it felt as if the only thing missing was the proverbial kitchen sink. It is not a pretty sight. Thankfully, many school districts do not cram that many on a school bus, we had approximately 55 students onboard that day. This means there were still a few seats that had three students sitting in them.

Now, there are a few things that happen when you get that many people on a bus at one time. First of all, the noise level increases exponentially and the students do not like to sit in their seats until the bus is ready to take off. Sometimes even after the bus has taken off they do not like to remain seated. Of course, I had just finished getting my CDL, so I was all about the rules and discipline. My friend Al did not seem to mind the chaos that was surrounding him. Therefore, I decided to take control of things, get the students to sit down and lower the noise level to a duller roar. In my very best bus driver voice, you might find this hard to believe, but for a small person, my voice is very big, I told the students to sit down and be quiet, so we could depart. Whence from the back of the bus in an equally loud voice, a girl shouts, "Sit the fuck down and shut the fuck up." I do believe my mouth dropped to the floor! When I recovered from my momentary shock and returned my jaw to its' rightful place, I responded, "Excuse ME?" It was at that point that the young person barking obscenities at me looked up and realized that I was not the middle school student she thought I was, but an adult. The shocking revelation on her face was absolutely priceless! I had no idea at the time of the incident that the girl hurling the colorful expletives would turn out to be a girl from our neighborhood. And so it began—the wheels of the bus definitely went round!

CHAPTER 1

Once in a Blue Moon

Not long after my very first jaw dropping moment, I was treated to another. I was waiting in the lineup at the high school with my middle school kids in tow. The busses filed in, end-to-end, meaning, that the front of the bus, was pulled up close to the bus directly in front of me.

The bus in front of mine was quite full and, as expected, the rear of the bus was the first section to fill up. Then, IT happened—that is right—IT happened. Right before my very eyes and without warning, out of the blue and in broad daylight, four asses appeared in the three rear bus windows of the bus directly in front of me. Not one, not two, heck, not even three, but FOUR full moons.

Once again, I found my jaw back on the bus floor. Adding to the amusement of the scene playing out before me was the fact that I had announce the entire event taking place on the CB radio, to inform the driver in front of me, what was happening on her bus. This meant that not only the driver in front of me heard the radio transmission about what was taking place, but the entire fleet of busses, base, and a host of other public entities as well. It was difficult enough for me to tell the driver in front of me what was happening, let alone to do so while holding back an array of flippant wisecracks and stifling a laugh that was just bursting to come out.

In those early months of driving, I found that my jaw must have had an obligatory number of times it had to hit the bus floor, in order to obtain some unknown status.

Blessedly, my first few weeks driving solo was done on a short bus, bus number 32. The capacity of which was only 30 passengers. This helped to dramatically reduce my jaw dropping episodes. The route itself was probably less than an hour in length. It was on a street in a section of the town where a large bus just did not do well, a no outlet street with very little room for a full-sized bus to maneuver around on. It was a beautiful area and a very picturesque setting, with lovely houses that lined the street. That one street just happened to fill that little bus to capacity. It was a perfect fit and I, of course, was more than happy to accommodate.

The start of my first full school year, I was shown no mercy. I was pulled from the comfort of the cute short school bus with the pretty little street and the easy little route and thrown into the world of sub-bus driving.

The school district I worked for was relatively small, but adequately equipped, considering the city we lived in numbered about 15,000. While we were not completely rural country bumpkins, we certainly were not a large city either. Aurora is situated about 45 minutes southeast of Cleveland and 30 minutes north of Akron. A charming small town far enough removed from the bustle of the big city, but closes enough to get to the action.

CHAPTER 2

Truth Be Told

From the time, I earned my CDL and the Kent Barker stamp of approval, until the end of the school year was only about six-weeks. I would have the entire summer to contemplate my return. Ha, that took all of about two seconds! I was hooked! I found where I belonged and absolutely loved school bus driving!

It was in Aurora where our son, Dominic, began his education and would be starting and ending his day on a school bus. I believe I was the odd parent out, when it came time for school to begin. There were no tears. I am not sure who was more excited that he was starting school, Dominic or me. I guess I just did not view it as a negative nor did the experience make me nostalgic that my little boy was growing up, that would happen—much later. I also knew that, in general, I had a very positive school experience growing up and was excited that Dominic would be starting his educational adventure! It is difficult to feel sad, when there is nothing but joyful enthusiasm oozing from your child. Then, combine that with the fact that the day he started was a bright sunny cheerful morning; you could not help but feel his joy, excitement, and enthusiasm, and not be positively affected by his abundant exuberance.

And so it began, walking Dominic down to the bus stop to get on the bus and being there to greet him when he returned. For many of us with boys, learning about what their day was like was a little like pulling teeth. How was your day? "Great." He would respond. "What did you learn?" I would ask.

"Nothing much," was his typical response.

Frankly, that is largely how many of our conversations went. Occasionally, however, conversations would become far more animated and I would hear some rather colorful storytelling. More often than not, most of the colorful antics and more interesting conversations happened, none other, than on the school bus. Some of the antics and conversations did not always make me happy, nor gain my approval; however, they did promote dialog and created some lively topics of conversation at home. One such conversation comes to mind.

Generally, Dominic would come home with a smile on his face, come to think of it, more often than not; there is a smile on Dominic's face. That day, however, was different. Not only was he not doting a smile, I could tell from the look on his face that he was very close to tears. I proceeded to ask him how his day was and got the usual response of "fine."

"What did you do?" I asked.

"Not much," he responded.

"Well then, why the sad face?" I asked him.

"Mom?"

"Yes, Dominic?" I said.

"Ethan said, 'There's no such thing as Santa Claus.' He told me."

My heart dropped. Dominic was only five and this was not what I had been expecting, at all. Now, Ethan was a fourth grader and at that moment, not my favorite neighborhood child. He was a bit of a know-it-all bully who did not have much time for the likes of a kindergartner and as it seemed, Dominic in particular. So begrudgingly, we proceeded to have the Santa Claus conversation.

"Is Santa Claus real?" asked Dominic.

"What do you believe, Dominic? Do you believe Santa Claus is real?" I asked him.

Deflection, nice parental defense huh? He was very quick to respond to the affirmative that Santa Claus was real. Whew! Close call—minor bullet dodging avoided. I relaxed thinking that particular conversation was over and we could save that conversation for another time. Wishful thinking on my part, about a half hour later, he came back into the kitchen with huge crocodile tears streaming down his little face. "Mom, you've got to tell me the truth. Is Santa Claus real?" He sobbed.

Great! Now, I was faced with a choice to make, which was not really a choice at all. I hesitated for only a moment before sharing, or rather confirming Ethan's story. So with a calm resolve that I did not feel, I proceeded to share the story of Saint Nicholas and through the spirit of giving that we emulated that tradition. That explanation seemed to appease him until once again, I was faced with a crocodile, tear filled faced, little boy with one more inquiry, only four words. "The Easter Bunny too?" He asked. His whole little world seemed to be unraveling with each new revelation and I had to be the one to unravel it. It was not my favorite day as a parent. With each tear that spilled, I found myself closer and closer to wanting to choke a certain fourth grader and quickly discovered that the school bus, though a delightful service, and generally a positive experience would, at times, offer up some benefits that I was not always fond of.

CHAPTER 3

Post it

While I was in the process of training, but before I obtained my CDL, I had the opportunity, on a number of occasions, to work on the bus as an aide. Assisting drivers on various routes, depending on what the needs were at the time. Typically, I was placed on a special needs route or on occasion a kindergarten route that was experiencing behavioral issues. As was the case on this particular day, I was asked to help. I told my supervisor, Nancy, that I would be happy to help, as long as she would ask Dominic's regular driver to bring Dominic back to the transportation department instead of dropping him off at his assigned stop, since I would not be there to receive him. He was, after all, just a kindergartner himself. Nancy agreed to my request, so I took off to do my aiding thing. When I returned, I went directly to the supervisors' office, to pick up Dominic. When I entered Nancy's office, I did not see Dominic and asked her where he was. Nancy took one look at me and her face went ashen. She had forgotten to ask Mr. Bill, Dominic's regular driver, to bring him back to the transportation office. Therefore, Dominic was let out at his regular stop, about 45-minutes prior to my return to the transportation office.

My heart sank. I walked out of the office listening to my supervisor apologizing profusely in my wake. In a panicked rush, I made the 10-minute drive home, in roughly five minutes, bursting into an empty house. I got on the phone, my panic rising, calling my neighbors to find my child. It only took two calls to find out where he was and that he was indeed, safe.

I rushed over to where he was and hugged him tight. At that moment, he looked at me, like I was daft and with a puzzled look on his face he said, "Mom, I left you a note telling you where I was."

"What note?" I said.

His proclamation, surprised me, and I told him that I did not find a note.

Now, my curiosity was piqued. My son was only five and, well, not much of a writer—or, so I thought. We walked home, hand in hand. I was one very relieved mom and I was with one very unconcerned child. When we walked into the garage, he pointed to a post it note that had fallen from the garage entry door to the floor, he picked it up and handed it to me, saying, "Here's the note I wrote you."

It was indeed, a note. I wish, with all my heart that I had kept it. If anyone, including myself, glanced at that note, without paying attention to it, they would have thought it the scribbles of a five-year-old child, but upon further inspection, and after reading it phonetically, this is what the note read:

I m et knrs hos

Allow me to translate for you. "I am at Conor's house."

It was simple, sweet, and to the point. WOW, was I impressed. I did not realize it at the time, but looking back, that was pretty cool.

My year of substituting flew by and the following school year, I was offered and accepted a full-time route—insert yet another major happy dance! YEAH ME!

Dealing with the mischievous antics of my kids is just one element of the job to be acquainted with. Sometimes, what starts out as something that was intended to be a harmless mischievousness prank, ended up taking an unintended turn for the worse. Such was the case in my next few stories.

CHAPTER 4

Super Sticky Situation

It has been stated, on more than one occasion, that if you are transporting middle school-aged children, you may be required to carry a hazmat endorsement. The following story is a good representation as to why it is a good idea.

In the early part of the school year of 2002, while driving for Aurora, I had a particularly mischievous eighth grade student named Ben. He was easily on the plus side of too cute for his own good and he knew it. He was popular with all the girls and generally tolerated by the guys on the bus. He made a habit out of torturing the sixth graders on the bus. For some reason, he always seemed to be the first person to board the bus. Lucky me. Then, the rest of my riders would start to meander onboard. As a group of sixth grade boys were entering the bus, Ben told them he had some sour candy that was amazing and that they should give it a try. The sixth graders were eager to participate.

25

By participating, it seemed like a win/win all the way around. I mean, after all, an eighth grader was talking to them and wanted them to try something. Man, it does not get much better than that. However, when something seems too good to be true, it ends poorly.

The two sixth grade boys boarding the bus were wooed into trying the candy that was being offered to them. Ben had some instructions as to how they were supposed to receive and eat the candy. They were told to hold out their index finger and when they did, Ben proceeded to put a liberal amount of the liquid candy on the tip of the boys' index fingers. While doing so, they were instructed on how they should taste the candy. They were instructed to smear the liquid candy on their lips and then lick their lips. The boys eagerly went about doing as they were instructed, only to find out that what they were actually putting on their lips was not candy at all, but Super Glue.

Oh dear, that was a mess. Ben, not only Super Glued® the boys' lips and got the boys to ingest the Super Glue®, which, by the way, contains formaldehyde. He also Super Glued® a girl's backpack to one of the seats, so when she went to pick up her backpack to leave, it ripped not only the backpack, but also the seat covering the backpack was sitting on.

Needless to say, I had more than a couple of angry parents after that little episode. Ben's parents were contacted, and he or rather his parents were made to compensate the damages that occurred not only to the girls backpack, but also the repairs needed to the seat cover on the school bus. Ben also received a well-deserved, unplanned vacation from both the school bus and school.

The quick reaction of the sixth grade boys realizing they had been duped largely saved them from suffering any serious ill effects of having their mouths Super Glued.

CHAPTER 5

Bubble Gum Mayhem

I had always believed that if I were ever going to receive a death threat from a student, it would come from one of my high school students or possibly from a middle school student. Never, ever, would I have guessed that my one and only death threat, to date, would come from a second grade boy? Yes, you read that correctly, a SECOND grade boy.

It was a beautiful sunny afternoon when the kids were boarding the bus that day. Jesse boarded the bus and while doing so, I noticed he was chewing a rather large wad of gum. Due to choking hazards, it was commonplace for many drivers, myself included, to request students to remove the gum from their mouths and dispose of it in the trashcan on the bus. Which, is precisely what I asked Jesse to do. When this type of request is made, it is usually met with varying degrees of protest. For Jesse, however, it was as if I had asked

28

him to sever his arm. He made quite a production of storming up the aisle, then pulling the oversized wad of gum from his mouth and expressly and forcefully tossing it into the trash. After which, he proceeded to make his way under the seats, firmly attaching himself to the frame of the seat with a death grip and absolutely no intention of letting go. He had no intentions of getting off the bus floor anytime soon and remained rooted to that spot. Nothing I said was motivating him to change his position. It was at that point, that I enlisted the help of my supervisor.

The school, where I was picking up students, was located adjacent to the location of where all the busses were stored in the evening and the location of the transportation building. In the beginning of the school year, you would often see our supervisor observing, organizing, and helping, where necessary. On that day, I was interested in the helping portion.

Sam was the supervisor, at that time, and came to our small school district from the Youngstown area. A young, small, soft-spoken, Italian man—HA! A soft-spoken Italian man, now, that is an oxymoron, but it was true. He came to my rescue that day and to my amazement, coaxed Jesse out from under the seats with relative ease and pretty darn quick, I might add! As Sam fished Jesse out from under the seats, he started to seat him directly behind me. I objected and requested that he seat Jesse on the passenger side of the bus, in the first row, so I could see him. Sam complied with my request and ushered Jesse to the seat reserved for my very special friends.

Now, there was a reason that I did not want Jesse directly behind me. We had an incident that occurred on one of our special needs busses, shortly before this event took place. A special needs student chocked one of our drivers with the driver's seatbelt, from the seat directly behind the driver. I was not up for a copycat performance.

With Jesse in his new, very special reserved seat, we were ready to depart to the next school to pick up more students, before taking them all home. We had just left the school property, when Jesse got up out of his seat, walked up next to me, standing next to the steps of the bus. He looked at me and said, "When I grow up, I'm going to get my dad's gun, set this bus on fire, and kill you and everyone else on it."

Well all righty then! Um...what exactly do you say to that but—PSYCHO! No, I did not call him that, but I was certainly thinking it.

Now, not only did I not want Jesse behind me, I did not want him on my bus at all! Very calmly, I radioed base and asked them to contact the school and have them meet me when I arrived, to remove

Jesse from my bus. Somehow, when Jesse said this, the threat seemed real. It was way too thought out for my taste and thoroughly disturbed me! The school removed Jesse from my bus and that evening, I filled out an incident report.

The next day, I met with the principal, the teacher, the guidance counselor, and one of Jesse's parents. Jesse's mother had the audacity to tell me that her child would never say something like that. Huh, that is odd; there was a child on the videotape, of this incident, that sounds and looks exactly like Jesse. What are the odds? Interestingly enough, showing the parent the video evidence was not an option. It infringes on the rights of the other children on the bus. However, the incident was documented and the child was removed permanently from my bus. That must have been some piece of gum. Bazooka, perhaps?

CHAPTER 6

The Wheels of Change

Ahh, my first year with my very own bus with my very own route! What could be better than that? I spent three more years with that school district, still loving my job and all it entailed. Things were about to change, in a very big way.

In the fall of 2004, my life and the life of my family was altered in a big way. The company that my husband was working for was purchased by an Italian based company whose North American headquarters was located in Mason, Ohio. Mason is a northern suburb of Cincinnati.

Our new home search led us to Centerville, Ohio. The community was a little further north than my husband wanted to go, but the school system had everything we were looking for, including an orchestra program that started in the fourth grade.

This feature was a major consideration, for choosing to settle in Centerville, Ohio.

I knew I wanted to continue driving school bus and to me, it made sense to drive for the community I was going to live in. Therefore, when we settled into our temporary corporate housing, I set off to find the Centerville transportation department.

Wow! All I can say is "Well Toto, I have a feeling we're not in Kansas anymore." I came from a school district that had a fleet of 40 busses; this district had nearly four times that. It was one of those good news, bad news scenarios. The good news was that I would get to start doing what I loved to do again. The bad news, I was once again, going to be thrown back into being a sub driver. Back to the grind of driving a new route, on a different bus, with different kids—daily. I was once again back to feeling completely clueless.

CHAPTER 7

I Know a Shortcut

Shortly after I started driving for Centerville, I was called upon to drive a particular route that transported both public and non-public schoolchildren. This particular route had me driving for a Centerville Elementary school and for Incarnation, a local Catholic school for grades kindergarten through eighth. The neighborhood plat that I was driving in was in a small development where most of the street names had a creek attached to them. For instance, there was Shady Creek, Silver Creek, Peachcreek, and so on. Being new to the area, it was not difficult for me to get turned around and I found myself in precisely that situation. One of the street signs was missing. This became a minor occupational hazard, making it easier to run-a-muck, so to speak. I called into base for some assistance on how to remedy my situation and get back on route. Though I do not remember the exact conversation it went a bit like this, "47 to base," I said.

"Go ahead to base." They responded.

"I've made a wrong turn and am unsure as to how I can get back on track. I'm in need of some assistance, please," I plead.

"Sure, we'd be glad to help. What's your location 47?" Now, I am thinking REALLY! What is my location? You are joking right?

"Well, I'm on one of the Creeks, though I'm not entirely sure which one because the street sign is missing." What I really wanted to say was *I'm up a creek without a paddle!*

Meanwhile, the natives were getting restless and the comments started flying. "Are we ever going to get home?" said one. "I'm hungry!" protested another.

"How much longer are we going to sit here?" yet another child lamented. Those were just a few of the choice comments assaulting my ears. A barrage of others was not far behind.

Base was struggling to assist me, not because they did not want to help me, but mainly because I was unable to give them my location. I decided to handle things a bit differently, which was to ask the children how to get back on track.

An older girl, sitting in the back of the bus, said that she knew what to do and would help me out. Relief washed over me. That relief was short-lived when she started polling the other students onboard "Who thinks we should turn left, raise your hand?" She asked them.

OK, this was not going as I had hoped, nor was I going to go with CONSENSUS driving. I quickly asked again, if there were any other students who could assist me on getting back on track. An eighth grade boy said that he would help and proceeded to give me directions. I thought things were going well. He seemed to know exactly where to go. We arrived at the stop and he proceeded to get up and leave.

"Is this the next stop on the route?" I asked him.

"No," He said. "I needed to get home. I have things to do and who knows when that would have been, with you driving."

Now, not only was I beyond frustrated, but I could now add angry to that list. Out of desperation, I asked one more time if anyone knew the way Ms. Linda drove her route, not directions for their houses, but the actual ROUTE. A quiet, soft-spoken, third grader, raised her hand and said that she knew how Ms. Linda drove and she would help me.

To say I was skeptical was an understatement! However, I did not have much of a choice; therefore, I decided to give the student a chance. Well, low and behold, she not only knew how to take me to the next stop, but she knew every turn and every stop thereafter. It just got better. Not only did she get me through the majority of the route she did not get off until just before the end of the route. Oh, bless you child! If getting up out of my driver seat and hugging that child were not frowned upon, I would have done it, right then and there.

I discovered early on, what my preferences were, with regards to which age group of children I preferred to drive. They turned out to be vastly different than I had originally anticipated. Before I had any experience driving for any of the different age groups, my first thought was kindergarten. I was certain that that particular age group would become my favorite, by far. They would be the ones to capture my heart and give me the least amount of grief while driving. WOW! I could not have been more wrong. I believed that my interaction with the high school students would be the bane of my existence—again, way off the mark with that line of thinking too.

I quickly discovered it was the kindergartners who proved to be most challenging for me in every way! I would like to say that the high school age group is my favorite, but that too would be remiss. I honestly cannot say which group, aside from kindergarten, is my favorite. Mainly, because the remaining groups have so many qualities that I have thoroughly enjoyed.

My elementary kids keep me thoroughly entertained on a daily basis. My middle school students, though challenging, I find completely engaging and my time with them is rewarding, and my high school kids truly are amazing. I enjoy each separate group for a multitude of reasons.

CHAPTER 8

Kinder-garbage

Kindergarteners, could you ever find a more adorable group of children on the planet? Generally speaking, this is a true statement and for many of my colleagues, this particular age group, for them, is by far and large their absolute favorite. I, however, have a different opinion entirely. As a driver, I affectionately refer to this age group of children as kinder-garbage.

Now, before every parent of a child this age goes and freaks out, please allow me to explain. It is quite simple, really, they LEAK. Oh! It is not just the teary-eyed water works that occurs, but also the leakage from every orifice. When the school year begins, the water works start. It is not just the kids that leak, but the parents too! Then, when the children are exposed to all the new germs from their classmates and classrooms, green goo and projectile vomiting, the nose and mouth becomes new leaking locations, then, periodically throughout the year, just for good measure, bathroom accidents—like I said every orifice!

Adding to the charm of this age group is the children's amazing ability or should I say inability to remain seated. While driving down the road and glancing at my students via rear-view mirror, I feel like I am watching a version of whack-a-mole. If you are not familiar with the arcade game to which I am referring, let me provide a visual for you. One by one, though sometimes more, the little darlings pop up in their seats and you see their tiny little faces shoot up over the barriers that are there for their protection. Now, picture these little heads popping up in rapid-fire succession for the duration of the bus ride. The requests of the driver for the children to remain seated generally falls on deaf ears. Or, it could be, that after requesting them to remain seated for the—oh, I do not know how many times. By this time, I have lost count. I, generally, give up or my voice gives out, whichever comes first.

Here is a request from me, to you. Please, do yourself, your child, and your child's driver a favor. When your child is ready to commence with their educational experience, please prepare them for that experience with this basic information, including, but not limited to, their name, their full address, their telephone number, and, your actual name. This may seem like standard knowledge that all five-year-olds know; trust me, this could not be further from the truth. The following is an example of a conversation on a kindergarten bus. It goes a bit like this.

"Dwiver, you passed my howse," unshed tears threatening to spill at a moment's notice.

"I did? Where do you live?" I ask.

"In...Sa...sa...sa...Cennaviwl," big tears, now and gasping for breath.

"Which house is yours?" I ask.

"Da...da...da...bwick one with the bwack shudduhs."

Great, that narrows it down to only 20,000 possible choices.

"What's your mommy's name?" I ask.

"Mawhahahamee!" This poor child is now inconsolably sobbing, gasping for air, with their shoulders going up and down, in spastic fits.

Oh, the agony of that journey, you do not know who to feel more sorry for myself or the child. It is heartbreaking seeing these little bitties cry. Well sometimes, it is annoying, but mostly, heartbreaking. They feel helpless. You feel, well— on the verge of killing yourself. Okay, that may be a slight exaggeration, but—meanwhile, some parent, somewhere, is about to lose it, because their child is a whopping ten minutes late. And NOW, when you do arrive, it looks like you just got done torturing their kid. Adding to the frustration of the moment, you thought you had their child calmed down, breathing semi-normally, with only the occasional gasp of air, now returns to a full-blown hysteria the moment they lay eyes on their parent.

Visually, when the parent sees their child getting off that bus, sobbing uncontrollably, you just know they are killing you with their death ray stares and you do not even want to know what kind of revenge they are plotting in their mind. But hey, just think, you get to do this all again, tomorrow— all of this is done, of course, with a smile. ☺

So please, for your sake—whom am I kidding, for my sake and sanity please teach your kids their address and your name before they start riding the school bus.

CHAPTER 9

Peek-a-boo

I generally feel very accomplished on the first day of school when I have completed my routes, for the day, and I have no surprises and no stowaways, not the case when I drove kindergarten, the one, and only year, I drove kindergarten.

Sometimes, when you choose a route at the beginning of the year, they are subject to change. Which may include an additional school added to your route. These practices are fairly common and I have since become accustom to having add ons to my route, shortly after the school year begins. During this particular year, I was given a portion of a kindergarten route, to alleviate an overcrowded route that was arriving tardy to school in the mornings. I have mentioned it before, but I will say it again—KINDERGARBAGE. Do not let those sweet, beautiful, innocent looking faces, fool you; they terrify me. I almost feel as if I were Arnold Schwarzenegger in *Kindergarten Cop*, a 1990's movie about a tough cop masquerading as a kindergarten teacher to catch a drug dealer. I could completely relate to how he felt. Well, not necessarily the whole tough cop thing or masquerading as a teacher looking for a drug dealer. Ok, I guess I could not completely relate, but I totally got how they rather freak you out.

I had one adorable child onboard that year. I wish I could recall his name, but I cannot...hmmm, maybe a repressed memory that I am blocking for some reason. Sounds like a great therapy session. Anyway, this little guy was beyond cute and had just moved here from India. He did not speak English, nor did either of his parents. They would walk Amir—oh my gosh—that is it, Amir. They would walk Amir to the bus every morning, his mother would smile, and wave, very sweetly, Amir would look at me with his huge brown eyes and enormous smile and go to sit in his assigned seat. Which, never lasted very long. Shortly, after we left his stop, one of the other kids onboard would tell me that Amir was crawling on the floor under the seats again. When we arrived at school, we would wait for the schools signal for the children to be released and I would wish each of my kids a good day as they departed the bus. When the last child departed, I would walk to the back of the bus to make sure that, no child was onboard or that no child left any of their belongings on the bus. On this day, as I was walking to the back of the bus, checking the seats, as usual, from out of nowhere, this adorable little shit jumps out from underneath one of the seats toward the back of the bus and yells "BOO." I am sure my reaction, from being so startled, could very easily have ended up on an episode of *AFV (America's Funniest Video's)* and quite possibly a winner. Amir found my reaction so amusing that he hid on the bus at school, everyday from that day forward. It became a daily game that we played that made us both laugh. Amir only started riding my bus midway through the school year, so I only had him for a short time. But, oh, what an impression he left on me! When I close my eyes, I can still see his beautiful smiling face, his laughing eyes, and mischievous spirit. And I may have left some claw marks on the ceiling of the bus from being startled so badly.

If you do start driving this age group, beware! They have a knack of getting completely under your skin, tugging at your heartstrings, and warming your heart so completely that you just cannot help but love them! The guileless affection they shower upon you, their joyful nature, and the laughter and singing they effortlessly share is definitely contagious, making this age group rather hard to resist, regardless of leakage.

Throughout my first year with Centerville, I was probably on every route there was traveling to every school in and out of the district. I drove both special needs and general population including the *Zoo Crew*, as they were so affectionately called. These were the so-called problem children, which once you got the opportunity to get to know this group of young people, turned out that they really just had crummy home lives and were largely a product of their environment.

CHAPTER 10

Zoo Crew

Ah, High Schoolers—as I said earlier, many high school students avoid the school bus, like the plague. The ones who remain, for whatever the reasons, I thoroughly enjoy. My students are courteous, friendly, and generally really pleasant to be around. I share with them some of my more amusing stories that I know they would enjoy and in return, they reward me with some amusing tales of their own! Usually colorful, kind of crude or crass, but I am glad I am worthy of having them sharing anything with me! There are a few stories that vividly stand out in my mind.

My first route for Centerville City Schools' contained a shuttle from the High School to The School of Possibilities, an elementary school, and a middle school. The School of Possibilities is a bit of a last chance school for Centerville students. Some students had parole officers; others anger management issues, and still others who just seemed to do better in a much smaller, largely independent, online study curriculum. What this all means is what I stated earlier. Home may not have been very high on the happy meter for many of them. The students would ride the scheduled bus from their neighborhood to the high school and wait for a transfer bus to take them to the School of Possibilities. That year, my bus was one of the shuttle busses going from the high school to the School of Possibilities. It turned out to be quite an education for me as well that year. I learned about P.O.'s, elf boots, and dropping dirty, who was pregnant, who was in jail, and who was doin' who. I learned some pretty interesting slang that year, as well as some poor grammar habits.

Jerry Mills was one of those students. Jerry was a really funny, high-energy guy who loved to talk, sing, tease, and sometimes annoy anyone who would listen. Most people listened. It was hard not to. He really was a very likable person. Most mornings Jerry would go into the high school and get breakfast, which for Jerry, meant a breakfast sandwich or M&M cookies. Often, he would even bring some cookies for me to enjoy. I always appreciate when students bring me treats. I am especially fond of chocolate, so his treats were generally a breakfast of champions for me.

48

One morning, a few weeks into the school year, Jerry got on the bus looked at me and said, "Damn woman you're pretty hot for an OLD chick," a strong emphasis on old.

"Thanks—I think," was my response. That's how they get ya! How do you respond to that! I was not quite sure if I wanted to laugh or cry, if I wanted to kick or kiss him. When I recovered from my momentary lapse of shock, I really wanted to laugh aloud, but decided I better not!

The area where I waited for students to board the shuttle bus was located at the furthest, most eastern portion of the high school. There is a large picture window on the second floor of the high school overlooking the east end parking lot. Many mornings, Jerry, myself, and the rest of the gang were treated, to a couple that would go to the second floor stairwell where the window was located, and proceed to make out. The stairwell was well lit and most mornings, when I waited for all the kids to show up, it was dark outside. This made for a very revealing and somewhat entertaining show from two unsuspecting teenagers.

It really reminded me of that show *Mystery Science Theatre*. An old show, where two science fiction type figures would give incredibly funny dialog to a film that was projected in front of them while the actual sound was silenced. We proceeded to entertain ourselves in a similar fashion giving commentary as to what the two were saying in their exchanges.

Realistically, when I reflect upon that year shuttling those kids—young adults, I am truly grateful for the time we shared, the laughs we had, and the fond endearing memories they have given me. As for Jerry, he was a senior that year. He graduated and went on to college, not a customary outcome for this particular group of young people.

CHAPTER 11

I Do

Often, I find myself sharing personal stories with my kids. Generally, they have to do with the topic of conversation at hand and some anecdote that I have had that I believe they would appreciate. Most of the time, it is the high school students I share the majority of my stories. One particular spring day, I was sharing the story of my engagement. This story was prompted by a particular conversation that was happening at the time about lame prom proposals. I told them that I did not have a lame prom proposal, but that I did have a lame engagement proposal story to share. Therefore, in order to move forward with this story, I am going to have to go back and share my engagement story with you.

I met my husband in Sandusky, Ohio. Wait, that is another story all together, it involves a bar and several incredibly corny pick-up lines. Let us fast forward to when I was transferred from

Sandusky to a store located in Grand Forks, North Dakota, and away from someone I had started to care for deeply. As it was, Nick was offered a job in Minneapolis, Minnesota, so we were headed off in similar directions, but many hours apart.

I moved to Grand Forks, North Dakota in February of 1990. The day I arrived was one of the coldest days I had ever endured and stands out as one of the coldest to this day. Now that is saying something, because I am from Minneapolis, Minnesota and was no stranger to very cold winters! The temperature was close to 20 below zero. That would be standing air temperature, with the wind chill, it was 40 below, and something in my memory is telling me it was 49 below zero. Now really, when it gets that cold I do not really think nine degrees would make that great a difference, but I am reasonably sure that you could not even spit without having it turn to ice before it hit the ground. It also had me questioning what on earth I was thinking, moving to this God forsaken place!

Nick and I continued to communicate via telephone, letters, and cards. Wow, even as I write this that sounds so archaic! It sufficed and we kept things progressing forward, relationship-wise.

He made the five and a half hour trek north to visit later that spring. Previous conversations had indicated to me that his intentions were leaning toward taking the next step in our relationship, so I was not surprised when the topic of marriage came up and we verbally agreed that it was something that we both wanted. After that initial discussion, the topic really had not cropped up again, and I did not think much one way or the other of the topic not surfacing again for the next month or so.

Seeing that we were both in retail, living in different states, and he traveled about 50 percent of the time, it meant opportunities to share time together was limited not just by distance, but also availability from our work schedules.

A number of weeks after our initial discussion of marriage, I received a package via Fed-Ex, now, it just so happened that I was off that day and was available for the delivery. Imagine my surprise when I opened the box and found a dazzling engagement ring, no card, no explanation, just this beautiful ring. Of course, I knew exactly whom the ring was from and called Nick immediately, only to have his answering machine take my call. Later that day, Nick phoned me only to have my answering machine take his call, but this time he asked if I would marry him. So, I was engaged via FED-EX and proposed to on an answering machine. Talk about romantic! I must say though, if nothing else, it was a one of a kind proposal, and completely original—just like him.

This is the story I was recanting to a few of my high school students. Upon completing this little tale, Alicia looked at me and said "And you married him?"

"Yes," I said.

"And...you're still married to him?" She asked.

"I am," I replied.

"Oh, well, that is the lamest proposal I've ever heard!"

CHAPTER 12

Dance Fever

Okay, this story has a lot going on, so pay attention people! Do try to keep up.

I have a sophomore girl, we will call her Addie who has a brother, he happens to be a senior I will call him Bill. Now, Bill has a friend, also a senior, call him Don. They all lived in the same neighborhood and rode the bus regularly last year. Recently, however, Bill obtained a set of wheels, so Don only rides when Bill is not available to drive him, though Addie rides daily. Okay, are you with me so far?

On this particular day, Addie got on the bus and sat next to Don. Shortly, after we left the high school, the conversation turned to the topic of the prom. Being that Bill and Don are BFF's, sitting and conversing with an underclassman was not the torture one might think.

Addie looked at Don and said, "Bill is taking my best friend to prom, and you're taking me. That's the plan...and well, YOU are part of the plan."

At this point in the conversation, I could not help laughing at the entire scenario and then audibly laughed, when I did not hear a single protest coming from Don.

Huh! That has to be the most creative way I have ever heard of getting a prom date and not just any prom date, but a cute older guy. You ROCK Addie!

CHAPTER 13

Lip Smackers

The high school stories that I share, do not happen nearly as frequently as with my elementary and middle school kids, but when they do, they are usually priceless, and I was treated to one that still makes me smile, every time I recall it.

Trevor, a ninth grader, got on the bus one afternoon and was explaining to Michael, another ninth grader, why he was out of breath and running to catch the bus before it left.

"I was kissing my girlfriend and she had on this shiny, sticky, lip gloss stuff that was supposed to be strawberry flavored. I had to run back into the school and wash that shit off, cuz it was so disgusting—, and I can still taste it! That stuff was awful! What's wrong with plain old Chapstick anyway? I told her not to wear that stuff again!"

I could not contain myself, I laughed outright at that proclamation. I even offered him a wipe to

57

get rid of the remaining offensive lip-gloss, but alas, he did not accept my offer. So ladies, please get rid of that offensive sticky foul flavored lip stuff and stick to plain old Chapstick. Your boyfriends will thank you.

CHAPTER 14

Manic Monday

November 12, 2012, was a dark bleak rainy day. It was 6:38 a.m. I had just left the lot to begin picking up my high school students. The bus I drove at the time had tinted windows making the bus even darker than the morning was already. The route that I was driving had been altered to accommodate all the road closures and construction that was happening at the time. The first stop of the day was located on a street with no street lamps and no outlet, which then required me to turn the bus around with a maneuver in the industry we call a turn-around. It accomplishes exactly what the name implies.

Driving on a morning like this is challenging. Visibility is greatly diminished. The lack of light and the rain compounded the challenges. Now, I was going to add a backing maneuver to add to the excitement, because I really needed to add to an already difficult situation.

I began backing with all the certainty of one of my new trainees backing the bus for the first time. HA! The only thought that played repeatedly in my mind was *I can't see a thing!* My mirrors were completely rain covered, which mattered little considering how dark it was outside combined with the added darkness of the tinted windows on my bus. Determining where street and curb met was next to impossible. I had backed up to a point where I knew I had enough room to go forward and considering that I no longer felt comfortable backing, I chose to proceed ahead.

I was feeling reasonably good about completing the turn around and moving forward again, when I heard the unmistakable sound of metal meeting metal on my bus. It was truly an oh crap moment, and one that thankfully is a very rare occurrence for me.

Once something like this happens, we are required to report the incident to base. We do this by announcing it over the airwaves via our two-way radios. A moment most of us drivers dread doing. Mainly, because each and every one of my fellow drivers, the local police, and fire personnel, and any other curious citizens with a scanner set to that channel can hear all of the transmissions taking place. Nothing is worse than having to announce your mistake on public airwaves and nothing like a big old slice of humble pie to start your Monday morning off right.

There were a number of silver linings throughout this whole uncomfortable experience. I had no students onboard and with it being as dark as it was, I could not assess the damage done to the bus. I was asked if all my lights were in operation, which they were; combine that with the fact that I had no children onboard at the time of the incident. It was OK for me to proceed with the remainder of my route.

I set about picking up my high school kids though my mood now matched the weather. It is an odd feeling to continue driving after you have made a mistake like that. I cannot say that my driving changed completely, but I almost started second guessing things that moments earlier just came naturally to me. Turns were taken a bit wider and slower, backing was nerve racking, and my confidence, in general, was completely shaken.

I picked up and delivered my high school kids and had a few minutes before my next route began. Daylight was finally filtering in around me and I had my first opportunity to assess my handy work.

Being that I hit a street sign, I was expecting the damage to be up high. I was quite surprised when I got out and saw that the only damage was just before the rear bumper on the passenger side of the bus. The corner of the bumper was pulled away from the bus and just before that, there was a scratch. Not at all, what I was expecting. Most street signs are quite tall and being that I did not strike the sign going backwards, led me to believe that the sign was quite likely already leaning forward for me to catch it where I did.

When I arrived that afternoon to drive my P.M. route, the damage had already been repaired leaving only a scratch as a reminder of my close encounter of the street sign kind.

With my nerves on edge and my confidence still shaken, I got back on the bus to pick up my elementary kids.

My mood was dark and I was definitely feeling sorry for myself, but my kids needed to go home and it was still my responsibility to make that happen. So, off I went bad mood and all to my elementary school.

The kids got on the bus as they always do, though today, I made little effort to intermingle and converse with my kids, which is very unlike me. My mood went largely unnoticed by my kids and they carried on with their typical jovial liveliness. Now, Jake, who usually attends an after school program, was on the bus that afternoon and sits up front in the first seat. Other students were milling about before I asked them all to take their seats in preparation for the ride home. One of my fourth graders, Joe, was being a bit rambunctious and I told him that if he did not sit down and remain seated, he would be moved to the front for an entire week. Jake, of course, heard my threat, and said "Yeah, and he will have to sit with me."

I agreed with Jake and said that indeed, that is precisely what would happen.

Jake then proceeded to tell me "Actually, I kind of like sitting up front by myself especially in the morning."

I was curious as to why he liked sitting by himself and was just about to ask him that question, when Jake offered up his explanation by saying.

"In the morning, Adam, the child that sits across the aisle from him and I get to practice our dance moves on the way to school."

To which I replied, "Your dance moves?"

"Yes, it's where I perfect them for my peeps."

Just like that, a smile crossed my face and both my mood and my day had been brightened.

They do that you see they can make you smile even on a day when you thought a smile could not be found. My high school kids continued to pick me up that day.

Gina got on the bus and told me that she was going to have to devise a plan to sabotage Ian's, a senior's, car so he would have to ride the bus, once again. I objected to this little plan, and asked her why she did not ask Ian for a ride. She gave me a lame reason as to why that was not possible, but then, she proceeded to tell me that she was going to marry Ian some day and that he just did not know it yet.

Interestingly enough and not long after that conversation occurred, Ian, the said senior Gina had her sights on was involved in an automobile accident and was forced to ride the bus once again.

Ian got on the bus and said, "I'm back."

"I see that your back," I said. "What happened to your car?"

"Oh, didn't you hear about my accident yesterday?"

"No, I didn't hear about it. What happened?"

He proceeded to share his story. Meanwhile, Gina, the freshman girl with the enormous crush on newly returned said senior who, by the way, she plans to marry him—he just does not know it yet.

Who, also claimed she had been plotting various ways she might sabotage said senior's vehicle to bring him back onboard, discovered his presence. I thought she might swoon from the excitement of seeing him! For two entire weeks, Gina was in heaven. Though she never actually sat next to Ian in the afternoon, she was never far from where he was seated. I never quite understood why Gina never opted to sit with him, given the chance.

When Gina left the bus the first afternoon Ian resumed riding, she made a point to tell me as she was departing, "No sabotage required, must just be fate."

How cute was that!

Continuing with the uplifting cuteness of the day, as we were traveling down one of the streets near the school, there was a high school boy and girl holding hands and skipping down the street. The sight and scene of the young couple was just too cute for words. It was such a delight to see kids being kids. The young couple was living, enjoying the moment, and each other, not even realizing the impact their simple act of holding hands and skipping affected those of us fortunate enough to witness the sweet innocent act.

The mopey misery that I clung to throughout that day just melted with each passing moment and was extinguished just like that. I guess it just goes to show you that people do notice what you do and they do notice what you say and boy, can they make difference.

You never know when a child is going to say something that is going to melt your heart, make you laugh out loud, or simply irritate and annoy you. One would think that I would come to expect the unexpected, but when these precious moments present themselves sometimes you just cannot prepare yourself and I still find myself at a loss for words or staring drop jawed in utter disbelief at what is transpiring before me. Sometimes, it even takes some reflection time for the event that occurred to really sink in.

Policies and procedures vary from district to district and state to state. One of the local policies for the district that I drive for is assigned seating for grades K-8. Every driver will comply with this request, but most will go about it in slightly different ways. Some will separate boys from girls, having the boys on one side of the bus and the girls on the other. Others will assign youngest grades up front and have the older grades in back, etc. I am a younger kids up front, older in back kind of gal. When it comes to my middle school kids, it is similar, but I let them choose their assigned seats as long as my sixth graders are up front and the eighth graders get the back rows, most are happy and little more needs to be said. That is, until a parent calls and decides that their daughter should not be exposed to "that girl" because she is a bad influence, or their son does not get along with that child could you please move them? Interesting thing is, in most cases, the kids choose their seats and seat partners. Hmmm, I wonder who has the real issue with the assigned seat the child or the parent. Occasionally, you do come across an incident where it truly is necessary to make alternate seating arrangements for students, like in the case with one of my middle school students.

CHAPTER 15

Bully Bully

Jacob was a small package of dynamite! Small in stature with a really big personality, only most people did not appreciate Jacob's unique personality. Never short on words and usually ready to open up a can of whoop-ass!

It was clear to me that Jacob was not the most popular kid on the bus and I am guessing that his popularity in the neighborhood was a little on the slim side and quite possibly at school as well. I had Jacob all three years of middle school and had to watch some of the boys get more and more verbally abusive with him. It eventually escalated to the point where I had to not only get the school administration involved, but also a number of parents. Parents, please, please, please talk to your children about bullying. Verbal bullying is so destructive and so very hurtful!

Hearing children tell another child that no one likes them and everyone hates them, that no one wants to sit or talk to this child, and that they are "stupid," then ostracized because they participate in something that is viewed as "uncool" is beyond heartbreaking! The damage it does to the child is irreparable and talking to the parent of this child is equally heartbreaking. I could hear the helpless frustration the mother was feeling when I spoke with her.

I know what a tumultuous time middle school is, but NO child should have to endure that type of abuse! I implore you to talk to your children! Please teach them to respect one another.

Even if a person is challenging to be around, there are far better ways to deal with people than resorting to name calling and hateful rhetoric.

Sixth graders tend to be a bit on the squirrely side, it is just in their nature.

CHAPTER 16

You're Never Fully Dressed Without a Smile

Just when you think you have heard it all, you get on the school bus and you find out that once again, you are wrong. Indeed, you have not heard it all. For instance, while driving my middle school students home. I was at a stop. One of my students, Melody, got off at that stop and when she left, I made the comment to the student behind me that I thought that Melody was quite possibly the happiest child I have ever encountered and believed there was never a time when I did not see her smiling.

Well, Jacob, the student to whom I made the comment to, responded to me by saying, "I'm pretty happy most of the time too, I'm just not capable of smiling."

"Jacob," I said, "everyone can smile."

To which he replied, "No, I can't. I sat in front of my bathroom mirror for two hours and practiced and I just can't smile."

Now Jacob has a voice that carries, even on the noisy school bus. By this time, several other students overheard our conversation and were chuckling at the prospect of Jacob not being able to smile and he had me laughing at the prospect too.

I told him it was easy, you just lift the corners of your mouth in an upward motion, and voila, a smile is born. Jacob, however, is convinced that he is incapable of smiling. I am making it my personal mission to ensure that smiling is something that Jacob is not only capable of, but also one he becomes proficient at doing.

Of course, I do get to deal with the mischievous antics of my kids too. Sometimes, what starts out as something that is intended to be harmless mischievousness, takes an unintended turn for the worse and no good becomes of it. Such was the case in my next few stories.

CHAPTER 17

Where There's Smoke...

Most of my more exciting adventures happen on my middle school routes in the afternoon, when they are bounding with energy and sugar. Mischievousness occurs with every age and grade level. It has been my experience that my middle schoolers tend to tip the scales when it comes to mischief. The life and times of a middle school student, oh my! This particular age group can prove to be quite challenging. They are children who desperately want to spread their wings, exert a little more independence, and push every boundary— real or implied. These next few stories will demonstrate the lengths they will go to see exactly where those boundaries are and how far they can push them.

This particular event happened on a lovely autumn day. I do not remember the date, but forgetting that day or the incident is highly unlikely. I was driving and enjoying the beautiful day. Many of the bus windows were open and we were enjoying the sights and scents of the crisp autumn day. I made it known that I smelled something burning. However, did not think too much of it because of the time of year, and because burning is legal within the township portion of the district. All was quiet, never a good sign. Something was up, that much I knew, but the two things I could not determine were "who" and "what." I continued driving. I even completed the route and thought that perhaps I had been wrong and that there were no unusual events taking place in the rear of the bus. That feeling was short lived when I returned to the bus barn and had a dreaded purple note attached to my time card, indicating that I needed to go in and speak with George. Purple notes are generally not a good thing. While waiting in the queue outside of George's office to speak with him concerning the purple note, I could only speculate as to why I was called in. I had an inkling. My instincts were correct. There was something going on in the back of my bus. What I did not realize was the magnitude of the antics that were taking place in the back of my bus. After having my tape pulled, it revealed three of my more adventurous, thrill seeking, eighth grade boys removing the leftover pieces of paper that remain when you tear paper out of a spiral notebook. They collected these paper remains and decided to set them on fire with a butane lighter. There is nothing like setting something on fire, inside a school bus, transporting a load of students, with a combustible substance having the potential to set the entire bus in flames. Thankfully, there were no injuries or damage to the bus or students. The three boys received a vacation from both the school and from riding.

Shortly upon returning from their unexpected vacation, my adventurous eighth graders antics continued. It did not take long before Lex and Drew felt the need to test their boundaries a second time. No repeat performances for these two, no! They decided to branch out and try something entirely new and different, though the outcome had similar results. Once again, upon returning to the bus barn, I found that I was greeted by yet another purple note on my timecard. This time, however, I had absolutely no idea as to what it could possibly be about, only that I knew that it was not likely to be a pat on the back for being a wonderful driver. The conversation went a bit like this.

"Did you have a problem on your bus this afternoon?" asked George.

"Not that I'm aware of," I replied.

"I had a couple of parents call in and tell me that Lex and Drew downloaded pornography on their cell phones and were passing it around to the other students on the bus," said George.

"I had no idea that was taking place." I replied.

Oh my gosh,—I really was at a loss for words, another first for me. This was something I could not see or hear them doing. It was also something relatively new as we entered the age of smartphones that were capable of producing highly inappropriate media at the touch of a button. When our simple communication devices, morphed into the handheld computers with worldwide media capabilities and the popularity of social networks, it created a completely new phenomenon that became known as cyberbullying. Now, kids who were once able to escape the school-bullying scenario suddenly had no reprieve from it. They now have the potential of being bullied via text and social media 24-hours a day, seven days a week, 365 days a year.

CHAPTER 18

Bonjour

Throughout the year, I have the opportunity to take field trips with students. On this particular day, I was taking a group of eighth grade students to a local French bistro to celebrate three years of French language studies. There were about 50 young people who went that afternoon.

When we arrived at the restaurant, the children were asked to remain seated on the bus, so Mademoiselle Newell could give the children some final words of wisdom and assign each of the children their dining companions for their luncheon. Once she addressed the seating arrangements, she proceeded to ask her students one last question and impart one final bit of wisdom with them before departing. This was her question. "Now class, why do all French people hate American teenagers?"

Shockingly and without doubt or hesitation, every child on the bus chorused in response,

"Because we're rude and obnoxious." I could not hide the look of shock that was written all over my face, but what baffled and utterly dumbfounded me was when the children responded, in affirmative of her statement. Madam slightly redeemed herself, when she finished her thought by saying, "Let us dispel that notion and show them that we are both courteous and respectful."

CHAPTER 19

It's Just a Number

While my middle school kids were waiting to get off the bus, a few of them were discussing who was dating whom. One of their friends, Maddie, a sixth grader was dating Logan, an eighth grader. Now both of the boys discussing this topic were mortified that a sixth grader would be dating an eighth grader. "It's just so creepy!"

Being the curious person that I am, I asked them what was so creepy about it.

They both gave me a look, like DUH! How dumb are you? Rhetorical question, do not answer it! "She is in sixth grade and he is in eighth. It's just wrong!"

Huh, wonder what their response would be if I told them about the 14-year age difference between my husband and me? Whoa! Talk about creepy! Think that might just tip their creep-o-meter! Heck,

I am not even sure they would survive the shock of it.

CHAPTER 20

Internet Sensation

You never know what is going to inspire a child. They are always watching or listening. Sometimes, they are doing both. One afternoon in the beginning of the 2011-2012 school year, my new sixth graders were sitting up front and were enjoying the music that was playing on the radio. The song that was playing was called *"Tonight Tonight"* by Hot Chelle Rae. I know, I know. How could I possibly remember the exact song playing on the radio right at that moment and on that day? I will get to how I knew exactly what was playing in a moment. Now, the ride that afternoon turned out to be a rather enjoyable one. The kids were singing and in general, just in good spirits, which always makes the day ultra-pleasant. I finished driving, returned to the bus garage, returned the keys to their rightful place, and went home for the evening. For all intents and purposes, it was just another day at the office.

I returned to work the next morning and while I was walking out to my bus, I was stopped by my co-worker, Derrick, who asked if I had spoken with another co-worker, Cassie. Well, it was 6:15 in the morning and I had spoken to very few people at that time. He proceeded to tell me that it was imperative I speak with her.

"Why?" I asked.

"Apparently, you are on you tube," he said.

"What?" was my reply. I could feel my face turning 25 shades of red. "What are you talking about?"

"Yea, apparently, one of your kids took a video of you on the bus yesterday. Her daughter, Allison saw it on You Tube last night," Derrick replied.

"Holy crap, are you kidding me?" Now, my heart was just about beating out of my chest and a million thoughts were racing through my head. A couple of thoughts kept playing over and over in my mind. What could I possibly have been doing that would cause her to video me. Moreover, please, please do not let it be something that might embarrass the school district or me.

When I completed my morning route, I went home as fast as I could and searched in earnest for the now infamous You Tube video. I have got to tell you, when you are, how shall I say this, not exactly a technical genius—who am I kidding; I am the furthest thing from tech savvy you can get. Okay, my parents actually get that award, but at least they have an excuse! Anyway, with a great deal of effort, I came across the video. The worry was completely for naught! Thank you God, I was NOT doing anything to embarrass the district or myself. Yes, I was in the video. Yes, I was singing. But, unless you recognized the back of my head or knew the bus number I drove, there was very little of me to see or hear. The funniest part of the video was the look of utter shock or was it disgust – hmmm, I am not sure – on Victoria's face to see that I was actually singing the pop song. The music and Victoria's singing were easily covering any singing that I was doing! I was mainly relieved to see that my kids were sitting down and for the most part behaving, except for the videoing that was going on unbeknownst to me. And me, well, I was driving properly.

When I returned that afternoon and my starring You Tube video had spread, I went into Larry's, my supervisor's office and said, "Hey, Larry, no need to pull my tape, just get on You Tube, you can watch the whole event there."

He laughed and I went on my merry way. Well, news travels fast and it did not take long before I was being teased for that too. Go ahead, look it up, you know you want to. It really is quite lame; as

You Tube videos go. Interestingly enough, since that time, I actually willingly published a demonstration video for my driving students. Come to think of it, that too, would probably be put in the, quite lame category, more like intensely boring. Unless, you are interested in becoming a school bus driver, or, you need a sleep aid, then you might find it quite useful.

CHAPTER 21

First Day Excitement

I am not sure who gets more excited about the first day of school, the kids or myself. I would have to say that it is probably a toss-up. Though I do have a coworker that quite possibly may love this job more than I do, that is really saying something.

This particular coworker took it upon himself to write a welcome back letter, to all of his students and their parents at the beginning of the school year. I was really impressed with this idea and decided that I too, would write a letter to my students and their parents. Only instead of mailing the letters out, as my coworker did, I would distribute them on the first day of school by giving them directly to the children as they went home in the afternoon. So, that afternoon, as the children were getting on, I gave each of them the letter, that I lovingly composed and had approved by my boss before I distributed it. The younger ones took the letter without question and most of them just placed them in their backpacks adding to the stack of papers they had received earlier that day during school.

I offered the letter to one student and when I handed it to him. This was his response "What is this?" He asked.

"It's an introductory letter with some information about me and my background to share with your parents." I told him.

"Oh, Mrs. Mileti, I have had you as a driver for so long, I know everything there is to know about you. You can keep your letter." He told me.

Well, alrighty then, needless to say, that was the one and only time I wrote a letter of introduction for my parents. Apparently, they know absolutely everything about me and no further information is required. Maybe, I should have him enlighten me, because I am still clueless and still do not know everything there is to know about myself.

CHAPTER 22

Five Good Reasons

I do not know if any of you recall a Pepsi commercial that was on the air back in 1998, it starred a young girl named Hallie Kate Eisenberg. She was an adorable curly haired, brown-eyed little girl, with a sweet disposition and generally soft spoken. That is, until someone tried to serve her a Coke. Then, all bets were off. Her voice transformed from her sweet quiet singsong voice into a deep, gravely, menacing sounding mafia man with an attitude.

The moment I laid eyes on Sara, I immediately thought how much she resembled that adorable little girl from the Pepsi ad. When she spoke, it only solidified my opinion further.

Sara, aside from being adorable is petite, high energy, talkative, leaned toward being a tomboy, and almost always wore a smile type of girl. At the time, Sara was in second grade. Being that she was in second grade, she was assigned a seat near the very front of the bus. She also had a crush on a fourth grader.

The fourth grader's name was Joe. Now Joe, another high energy...oh heck it is elementary they are all high energy. Joe was a talkative, very tall, total sports enthusiast, and of course, a really cute kid.

Not too far into the school year, Sara would ask if she could sit with Joe, who sat three rows behind her seat. Typically, I would have Joe move up to where Sara was sitting as opposed to her moving back. More often than not, I was amenable to this request, if Joe agreed to move to where Sara was sitting. Here is a big shocker, he hardly ever said no.

The two of them together would generally trade every type of sports cards made. That morning the ride to school was no different and the two set about the business of trading cards. Midway through the ride to school, their conversation piqued my interest.

The generally soft-spoken tone that was customary for Sara was heightened "I'll give you five good reasons to stop that." She even had her hand in the air slowly curling each finger into a fist. You know, Lucy Van Pelt style.

To which Joe replied. "I'd like to see you try it." Let me remind you, Joe is a good foot and a half taller than Sara. This was NOT even remotely a concern for Sara; her response to Joe's taunt was given, only this time, in a far more menacing tone. "Just watch me!" I was half expecting to see her head spin around.

Until this point, I had only been listening to the exchange-taking place between the two children. After hearing Sara's last comment, I knew it was time to intervene with the escalating squabble. I calmly told each of them that, that type of talk was inappropriate...blah blah blah. What I really wanted to do was see my little spitfire, Sara, knock Joe's block off. Not that I ever want to see any of my kids get hurt or intentionally hurt another child, but Sara exhibited so much confidence and had absolutely no fear of a boy nearly twice her size. With that kind of confidence, she may just have been able to pull that one off!

CHAPTER 23

Filter This

Every now and again, you get a truly challenging child on the bus. Jesse was one of these children. Now, Jesse had no filter and I mean NO filter, whatsoever! He truly is a case of think it; say it, with little regard for what the outcome or the consequences may be for saying exactly what he was thinking. Now, sometimes I think he blurted out some things just for the shock and awe factor. Then again, I have been wrong before. The following are just a few examples of the verbal escapades I have been treated to for the three years I drove for Jesse.

In the beginning of the school year when I first started driving Jesse, he would get on the bus in the morning and before leaving the bus to go to school, would tell me "You're a terrible driver." Then, in the afternoon when driving home before getting off the bus, he would repeat the same statement he left me with that morning. Day in and day out, over and over, I would hear from Jesse that I was a "terrible driver." I would not respond and just let him talk, but after three weeks of being barraged with the terrible driver comment, I decided to ask him what made me a terrible driver.

It was in the afternoon and just like clockwork, Jesse got on the bus and once again stated, "You're a terrible driver."

To which I asked, "Jesse, what makes me such a terrible driver?"

He had become so accustomed to me not responding that I think I surprised him when I did ask. He looked at me, cocked his head and said "Hmmm," cocked his head the other way and said "Hmmm," again, head cocking, "Hmmm." This went on for about a minute until he finally said, "You drive too fast." Then, a boy from the row just across from him piped in and said, "Yeah, you drive too fast." Then several others repeated the phrase. I think they actually had me believing I was driving too fast. Interesting thing is from that day forward he never told me I was a terrible driver again.

Not too long after the terrible driver incident, Jesse was getting off the bus at his stop and told me he had a question he needed to ask me. I said, "Sure Jesse, what's your question?"

He said, "Where do babies come from?"

To which I responded, "Jesse, I think that is a question that would be better answered from your mom and dad." He says, "I already know. It's like this," with some serious Elvis Pelvis moves, Jesse proceeded to gyrate fairly graphically in front of me. Jaw dropping was starting to become second nature for me; I quickly recovered telling him that behavior was inappropriate and unacceptable. Laughter, of course, was welling up inside of me just waiting for the appropriate moment to let loose!

It did not take long for me to realize that Jesse was going to be a wealth of adventures over the next three years! It is entirely possible that driving that child long enough could have given me an entire books worth of adventures to share with you. So, let us continue.

CHAPTER 24

Just a Little Kiss

Before I knew any better, I allowed Jesse to sit somewhere in the middle of the bus. He had not yet earned his way up to the front seat, but all that was just about to change.

Jesse sat next to a darling second grader named Maddison. Jesse's shock and awe conversations were not reserved just for me; he was nondiscriminatory when dishing out his verbal antics. While enroute to school, Jesse informed his seat partner, Maddison, that if she did not kiss him he was going to get his dad's shot gun and shoot her. Talk about really wanting a kiss! Oh, do not get your undies in a bunch. The threat was taken very seriously and he got a long vacation from riding the bus.

Jesse returned after a number of weeks away and from that day forward had one of my special reserved seats for my very special friends. Many of us, myself included, thought that after Jesse's hiatus and move to the front would help to curb or possibly eliminate the verbal assaults. Alas, no! Jesse had only been admitted back on the bus for about two weeks when our next adventure began.

It was a beautiful spring afternoon and the elementary ride home was rather uneventful and kind of quiet. Just the way you like them, till you realize that that is the calm before the storm.

Have you ever asked what someone said? You think you know what you heard, but you want to confirm it? Then, once the question is out of your mouth, you knew it would be a mistake because you did not really want to hear their response again? Well, I made that mistake. I knew what I thought I heard Jesse say but stupidly asked, "What did you say?" I really should have known better than to ask that. What I did not expect was the following:

Jesse said, "nothing," which I knew was not true, but then again, so did about half the bus.

One-by-one like little popcorn balls, children started standing up and repeating exactly what he said. It went a little bit like this—"He said, 'Lick my balls!'" This phrase was repeated over and over again. At least a half a dozen times in succession by different children, Yep, I was right, that is what I heard.

If it is been a while since you have actually stepped foot on a school bus, then you may not know that many of them, if not all are equipped with cameras that not only record a visual, but provide an audio as well. Yes, this whole event was recorded.

I knew I was going to hear about this little escapade. I had no idea it was going to be so soon after it occurred. I did not even finish with my route that afternoon when I got a call on the radio asking me to stop in and see the supervisor. I did not even have to guess as to what the request for my presence was for. I knew exactly why I was being sent to the principal's office!

I walked into the supervisor's office and he asked me if I had a problem on my bus, to which I recited the whole scenario to him. He really did not have to ask, because several of the children onboard recanted the entire afternoon's events to their parents, who in turn, of course, retold their child's version of the story to George.

You may have guessed it; Jesse was given yet another vacation from riding the school bus. Again, ooh—there is a big shocker! This incident happened in springtime, so when Jesse was finally admitted back on the bus, I think there were only a couple of weeks left in the school year, which he did manage to get through with no additional escapades.

CHAPTER 25

Mother May I

In February 2013, Jesse decided to join us on the morning route. For whatever reason, Jesse had not been a regular rider either the a.m. or the p.m., but on that February morning, he was there. Many of the conversations taking place between the students occur while I am driving. It is not until I pull into the school parking lot that I get to participate in any of these conversations.

On this particular day, this is what I heard Jesse say. "Would your mother allow you to do that?"

Upon hearing that, I looked into my student mirror to see if I could see anything out of the ordinary. Nevertheless, when I looked, I saw nothing unusual.

A few minutes later, I heard Jesse proclaim "No, really! Your behavior is very distracting!

Would your mother and father honestly allow you to do that at home?"

Now, I was curious as to what was going on, but again, when I looked, I could not see anything. Finally, we arrived at the school and I turned around and asked Jesse who was bothering him and what they were doing.

He replied rather indignantly "Oliver here is squealing like a little girl," to which I stifled a giggle. I had gotten so good at tuning out what they were doing behind me that I did not even hear Oliver squealing like a little girl. Now, it was my turn to be bewildered! This was coming from none other than—Jesse, the aforementioned Jesse and all his antics was now questioning the behavior of another child? Wow! Okay, who are you and what did you do with Jesse? Talk about a dramatic turnaround! Jesse remained one of my very special front seat riders until I received a note from our transportation office with a message requesting me to phone Jesse's father at home.

I made my way to one of the office phones and made the call to Jesse's father. Mr. Baxter asked me how Jesse had been doing when he rode the bus. I told Mr. Baxter that I had noticed a significant improvement in Jesse's behavior when he rode the bus. After hearing my response, Mr. Baxter made a special request for Jesse. He asked me if I would consider allowing Jesse to sit with his fifth grade classmates, in the back of the bus. Initially, I declined his request. I was not as convinced as Jesse's father in his transformation. Mr. Baxter said he realized that Jesse had been a jerk (his words, not mine) in the past and understood my position, but that he truly believed that Jesse had matured and deserved another shot at being allowed to sit in the back with his friends. He preempted his statement by saying that if I agreed to move Jesse back and by doing so, he messed up, to bring Jesse back up front. I told him I would have to approve it with my supervisor, but I was willing to try it. I was reluctant, to say the least, but I gave it a go with the understanding that one mess up and Jesse would be right back up front with no chance of returning.

What a great pleasure it was to have Jesse show off his maturity and a very pleasant surprise for me as well! Jesse had really grown up and got to finish out the school year in the back of the bus with no further incidents. I do not transport to the middle school that Jesse would be attending the following year, so our adventures together ended. I know he is someone I will never forget, and his presence will be greatly missed. I will always treasure the memories he has been a part of!

CHAPTER 26

Easy Reader

For a couple of years, while I lived in Centerville, I belonged to a book club. One of the books our group decided to read was called *"Wish You Well"* by David Baldacci. It was a simple story set in the 1940's in the hills of West Virginia. It was typical for me to pick up our book club reads at the library and this book was no exception. This time, however, the only copy available was a large print edition. I thought nothing of it and checked the book out. Depending on the route you have and which schools you pick children up from, you sometimes have what we call layovers or time between routes before you pick up your next group of kids. Go on just about any bus and you will find all sorts of reading materials. It is a favorite pastime of many drivers. Often times, I would still be reading as the children started entering the bus in the afternoon.

On this particular day, as my elementary students were getting on the bus, I was reading my book. This school would let the children out by grades starting with the second and third graders and then the fourth and fifth graders. Brenda, one of my third graders, entered the bus and saw that I was reading. She looked at the book and noticed the oversized print, after which she came right next to me, put her arm around me, and very sweetly says, "Awwwwww are you reading an easy book? My little brother reads those at home all the time and he is five."

To which I replied, "Why yes Brenda, I am reading an easy book."

Of course, what I really wanted to say was I am trying, but there are not enough pictures in this book, so I am finding it way too difficult.

This leads me to a major bone of contention. As drivers, we have to deal with a number of parents from time to time, whose opinions transcend through their children and are repeated to the driver. Their opinions are that school bus drivers are lacking in competency and/or, intellectual capacity. REALLY! Are you kidding me? If you truly believe your school district's drivers are incompetent or intellectually challenged, why would you trust any of your school district's drivers with your child's life? Because folks, that is precisely what you are doing each and every day you put your child on a school bus. Please, take the time to find out who your driver is and what they did before they became a school bus driver. You might be shocked, in a pleasant way.

Since becoming a school bus trainer, or, On Board Instructor, I have had the pleasure of meeting and training many of our new drivers and learning all about them and their backgrounds. The diversity of this group is astounding. Our drivers range from retired policemen, firemen, military pilots, drill sergeants and colonels, retired executives, doctors, realtors, salesmen, and of course, mom's. All walks of life and socioeconomic backgrounds are included in this wonderful group of people and yes, even impressive arrays of academic backgrounds encompass the individuals I am proud to train and drive along side.

Now, children will tell you absolutely everything! So, if you do not want your children repeating what they see and hear, make certain they are nowhere near when you are saying or doing things that you would prefer not to be repeated.

CHAPTER 27

Just a Little Wiggle

On a day when we have an extended break like Thanksgiving or Winter Break, the students are generally very excited about getting home. To add to the excitement, the teachers or parents usually provide the students with lots and lots of sugar just before they get on the bus in the afternoon, which generally makes for very lively ride home. This particular incident happened during the afternoon route just before Thanksgiving break.

The students were boarding the bus as usual by grades. One of my fourth graders, Zander, boarded the bus and stated, "I'm so happy I'm going to wiggle my junk." He was NOT referring to items that he was carrying or things in his backpack that he wanted to shake. This particular reference was to his manhood, which he took from a song that was very popular at that time. Once again, it was rather difficult not laughing out loud. Particularly, when the statement being made was done so, by a nine-year-old boy. I did manage to refrain. Adding to the amusement on that day was when the song to which Zander was referencing started playing on the radio; that song being *"I'm sexy and I know it"* by LMFAO.

Two thousand eleven was the first year that I actually had a radio onboard. So listening to music while driving my bus was as new for me as it was for my kids. Typically, however, when the heaters and defrosters are on and the regular engine noise is happening, I can rarely hear what is playing unless the volume is turned way up. When the radio is turned up enough for me to hear above all the engine and fan noises, it is way too loud for any of the passengers. Therefore, unless I am stopped to let students on or off the bus or I am driving alone; the radio is rarely up loud enough for me to listen to regularly.

I arrived at Zander's stop and he and three other children got up to leave. Three of the students were singing the chorus to *I'm Sexy and I Know It*, when Jeremy, one of my third graders, made his way off the bus. He turned to face me and said, "Mrs. Mileti, that sowng is just so inapwopweot." If you have ever heard the song or seen the music video, you would probably agree the song is inappropriate. Now, seeing that a large percentage of the bus was singing the song, I knew that their exposure to the song was not a first, but I made an executive decision. Before I was met with any objections or confronted by irate parents for listening to inappropriate music on the bus, I would have to ban the most requested radio station and switch to one that was not quite as popular with the students.

CHAPTER 28

Cupcake Anyone?

A few shorts weeks later, and again, on a Friday afternoon just before Winter Break or, as I prefer Christmas Break, another child stole my heart. Before I get into this story, I must give you a bit of a background leading up to yet another very amusing moment on my bus.

A couple of days before break, Carl, one of my second graders, got on the bus and thrust a beautifully boxed gift into my hands and rather harshly stated, "Here! It's a cupcake! DON'T tip it over."

To which I replied with a somewhat perplexed and tentative tone "Thank you Carl." It was quite clear to me that this was a gift that he would have preferred not to give and was definitely one that his parents encouraged him to give. I thought little of the brief encounter until my Friday afternoon ride home just before break.

The students were enjoying music on the way home and were, in general, in very festive and uplifting moods, which make for a very enjoyable drive home. I shared some departing words with Carl as he was exiting the bus, you know the typical departure comments for that time of year...Have a wonderful break, see you next year, enjoy the holidays etc. etc. etc. He got off the bus, turned and looked at me. The response I typically get is, and, frankly the one I was expecting to hear was... "You too Mrs. Mileti, or Merry Christmas Mrs. Mileti." (Something we are not allowed to say anymore...could be offensive.... Sad but true.) This is another sore subject for me.

In this case, however, the response I received was "I just don't like you."

Hmmm. Well, I was not quite prepared for that response. How does one respond to a bold statement like that? I will tell you how, by doing the only thing I could think of. I ignored it, mainly, because I really was at a loss for words. That and Brandon, a fifth grader getting off the bus behind Carl was telling me how much he was going to miss me and that he needed a hug because it would be soooo long before he would see me again. This helped to pull my bruised ego off the ground from Carl's bold proclamation.

Once all my elementary students were delivered, I had time to ponder what had just transpired, and the more I thought about it, the funnier it became to me. Carl's blunt, acknowledgment of his feelings toward me, only preceded to endear him further to me. Probably not the effect he was hoping for when he said it. You see, Carl is a feisty redhead who likes to make those around him laugh and he is typically successful at accomplishing this goal. His singing and dancing antics are contagious and usually end up getting those around him to join in his silliness. You see, for me, happiness is infectious and those that promote happiness generally make me happy too.

When I conveyed this story to a few of my high school kids, they were appalled at the child's boldness, but when they realized that I was not hurt by his words, it became amusing to them as well. It also did not hurt that my husband and I used that "I just don't like you" line that weekend whenever we could. It made us both laugh each time the story or the punch line was recalled.

CHAPTER 29

Monday Monday

In the morning, while waiting for the elementary school to open their doors for the day, I have the opportunity to spend a few moments chatting with my kids. I generally ask them how their weekends were on a Monday morning and what they did, where they went, if it was busy or boring and so on. On this particular morning, I apparently did not ask the question soon enough for my Rene.

"Mrs. Mileti, aren't you going to ask me about me weekend?"

"Well, of course, I'm going to ask you about your weekend Rene. How was it and what did you do?"

"Oh, it was just great! I got to be with my grandparents and we went to Oktoberfest in Dayton." Rene proceeded to tell me all about Oktoberfest and what she and her grandparents did that day. Rene asked if I had ever had Ben and Jerry's ice cream, and did I know that there is actually a Ben and Jerry's ice cream store in Dayton? She informed me that her grandparents took her there for ice cream that weekend as well. Her excitement was palpable, her enthusiasm, and joy burst with each new thing she was telling me. In the meantime, however, my second grade boys were starting to get a bit rambunctious. I asked the boys to please sit in their seats. Josiah decided to help his seat partner, Alan, to sit by physically persuading him to do so and assisted him in the process. All the while, I am witnessing the encounter between the two of them. I knew that the exchange occurring between the two boys, rambunctious as it was, was a harmless gesture. I told the boys, "There's no pushing on the school bus, what are you thinkin'?

The two boys had no response to the inquiry. However, Jason, the boy sitting across the aisle from them was quick to respond in their defense. Without missing a beat, his reply was "What they're thinkin' is that they're boys and that's what boys do." So there you have it. That is what boys do! How could I have been so ignorant to that simple fact? After being enlightened by Jason's wisdom, Rene and I both proceeded to roll our eyes and laugh.

CHAPTER 30

Super-Size Me

I have mentioned previously that physically, I am a petite person. I am roughly five-foot tall and approximately 100 pounds. I tell you this; because my next story demonstrates that regardless of what size you are children see you in an entirely different light.

While my elementary kids were boarding one afternoon in the early fall of a school year, Kevin, a fourth grader was climbing onboard. I remarked to him how tall I thought he was getting. Through his confirmation of my observation, I gathered he had heard that comment numerous times before. Continuing with the dialog, I proceeded to ask him if his father was really tall. He said, "Yes, he is VERY tall...He's just a little taller than you are." Now, I am thinking to myself has this kid ever seen me stand up. I mean really! WOW! Never in my life have I ever been viewed as tall! Nevertheless, to Kevin, on that day, in that moment, I was tall.

Shortly after my conversation with Kevin, I asked another child, Joe, about a sub driver who drove my route on the previous Friday afternoon, while I was absent. I generally will inquire as to who the sub was and how things went in general. I try to ask a child, whom I believe will give me the most accurate account of the afternoon's events. The hope, of course, is that there are no events to recount.

"So, Joe, how was the sub last Friday?" I asked him.

"She was horrible!" he replied.

Surprised by his response, I continued my questioning. "What did the sub look like?" I asked.

Being that I trained many of the subs and knew all of them it was likely that I could figure out who the person was based upon his description. "She was about your age with dirty blonde hair, only not dirty blonde like yours." He said.

Wait—what? Now, I am not focusing on the rest of what he is saying as I am stuck on the dirty blonde comment. I am thinking to myself, um, what blonde? I have no blonde. I am nothing but dirty—

well, brown anyway that is unless he is referring to the umm...blonde ya...right...blonde. He was referring to, the naturally occurring grey highlights that were shining through the "dirt." Okay Joe, I get the picture! Could he have given me a clearer indication that a trip to the salon was definitely in order? I think not! Needless to say, I missed a good portion of the remainder of what he had to say. I really needed to talk to my stylist!

Later that afternoon, I learned the identity of sub, which by the way, was a man by the name of Jerry, who is a regular driver, who was assisting George, our boss, with other routes since his preschool route is not in session on Friday afternoons. This also meant that the person Joe was referring to was Jerry's aide. Centerville has bus aides on all their special needs routes. The person Joe was referring to as that "horrible" person, was Dana. To which I later found out that the reason she was so "horrible" was because she asked my kids to sit down and be quiet before leaving the school.— How dare she...!—That was something I made them do on a daily basis. Therefore, I guess that makes me equally as horrible. So much for getting an accurate picture of what happens on the bus while I am away.

CHAPTER 31

Mirror Mirror

At some point in our lives, we are taught that having a favorite child is inappropriate and potentially harmful to the less-favored child's ego. While this may hold true for my own children, I find it much more difficult to adhere to on the bus, therefore, do not. I try not to make it blatantly obvious, as to whom are my favorites, but I do have them. They exist for various reasons such as the cute factor, the personality-plus child, and the ones that just endear themselves to you by what they say and do.

David is one of those children who is not particularly loved by the other bus riders, but is one that I found completely endearing. My friend, David, was a second grader at the time and happened to be very talkative, somewhat argumentative, and a bit of a know it all. Because of David's physically active and talkative nature, his assigned seat was first row right behind me. The first two rows of seats on my bus are reserved for my very special friends and David was definitely one of my very special friends! When David got on the bus, he usually had a story to share with me about how his day went. Usually, I would hear if his clothespin managed to stay on green, which was not often, or what happened for his clothespin to be moved to red. Clothespins represent behavior. If a child's behavior in the classroom was acceptable, the said clothespin remained on green. If a child's behavior was less than desirable, the pin would be moved to yellow as a caution and if the behavior was disruptive or unacceptable, the pin would be moved to red, which usually meant a note or phone call home to the parent. On this particular day, however, the topic of conversation had nothing to do with clothespins. David had a far more pressing question to ask me when he got on the bus this particular afternoon. "Mrs. Mileti, do I look better with my glasses on or off?" he asked.

"Well David, I think you look just as good with your glasses on as you do with them off." I told him.

He shook his head at me and said, "I don't think so."

"Well then David, why don't you tell me what you think?" I responded.

"Well, when I go home and look in the mirror with my glasses off, I almost fall in love with myself." He replied.

"Really?" I asked.

"Yep, I almost fall in love with myself."

Wow! How was I supposed to look at David without laughing out loud hysterically? Which, by the way, is exactly what I wanted to do! Amazingly, I refrained, saving my bottled up laughter to share with my colleagues and family.

CHAPTER 32

Auto Response

Auto response, we are all guilty of it, we do it all the time. Take for example our typical greeting, "Hi, how are you?" Then, you expect the auto response in return. "Fine, how about you?" Meanwhile, the other person is half way down the block and probably could not hear you respond to the contrary. Do you ever really expect any other answer than then the typical auto response answer? There are times we do this and probably do not even realize that we are doing it. Such was the case for this next story.

Christopher, a fourth grader, was getting off the bus and clearly on autopilot when he walked by me and said, "Bye, love ya." He reached the bottom of the step and realized what he had just said to me. He turned around and put his hands in the air, like, oh boy, did I just say that, and did she actually hear me? All the while turning a unique shade of red that I am not sure even Crayola would have a name for. As he stood at the bottom of the stairs facing me, he stammered. "I mean...I mean...I mean.... Bye. I do LIKE you though."

I could not help myself...I could not even wait to laugh out loud!

CHAPTER 33

B-L-E-E-P

The day we return from one of our holiday breaks, the kids are usually quite subdued and the ride to school in the morning is unusually quiet. I am relatively certain that they are still asleep when they get on the bus that first morning back from break. Occasionally, I will forget this fact and for a brief moment think to myself, OK, who are these children and what did you do with mine! However, not to worry, it is generally short-lived and I can count on everything being back to normal the following day.

This exact scenario played out when we came back from break in January of 2013. Monday came and went. All three schools that I drive for were eerily quiet in both the a.m. and the p.m. And, as I stated, the reserved quiet on the bus would not last long and sure enough, the next morning, organized chaos resumed on my elementary route.

Alan was in his assigned seat behind me and shortly after I picked him up, he inquired as to whether or not I would turn the radio on. He said, "It's not Christmas anymore." Now, I realize that his comment sounds unusual, but shortly before the break, the Sandy Hook elementary shootings had just taken place and we had been asked by our administration to leave the radios off. I complied with what was being asked of me and left the radio off. In the days that followed the tragedy, you could not turn on the radio without being inundated with conversations about the horrible event. Needless to say, I did what I was asked to do.

Interestingly enough, the only questions or concerns raised were about why they were not allowed to listen to the radio. Of course, I made up some lame excuse as to why we could not listen to the radio, which prompted them to sing holiday songs, so it actually worked out kind of nicely. I love to hear the kids sing.

When I told Alan that indeed we could listen to the radio, he decided to announce it to the entire bus. "Hey everybody, we get to listen to the radio! And now that it's not Christmas, we can listen to music with dirty words in them." Well, that is just perfect! Okay, just so you know, dirty words to a second grader are sex and sexy. I do NOT let them listen to radio stations whose morning show personalities, topics, and content, from the likes of such people as say Howard Stern, Elvis Durand, or others like them. Having said that, I do play a variety station where they do play a lot of pop music and as many of us know, pop lyrics as of late have plenty of those two lyrics!

Speaking of lyrics, especially lyrics that you are unfamiliar with can be especially amusing on the school bus. Of course, it is even funnier when you know exactly what the lyrics are and the children behind you are singing something entirely different. On the other hand, when you yourself are unfamiliar with the words and are either making up your own lyrics or singing what you believe the artist is saying. In either case, the results are the same and generally quite amusing. In this next story, however, it was not necessarily the lyrics that were puzzling to my students, but the actual artist who was in question.

On a Monday morning in early April, I had the radio on while picking up my elementary kids. Brady, a second grade boy was listening to the song that was playing and asked his seat partner Josiah, "Is that Elmo singing?" His seat partner gave no response to his inquiry, so, I asked him if he was referring to the person singing the song on the radio. He said, "Yes."

"No, that's not Elmo, that's an artist by the name of Prince and the song he is singing is called *Kiss*." I replied.

From now on, when I hear that song, I will have a visual of Elmo rockin' out on his guitar and belting out, "I just want your extra time and your— kiss."

I found this story so amusing, that I came home and actually sent it in to the local radio that played the song earlier that morning. I never actually believed that anything would happen with the short correspondence I sent off, but low and behold, as I was driving the kids one morning, a number of days later, they actually started reading the story on line. Imagine my surprise. I am not sure if any of the kids heard the story being recanted over the airwaves, but it put a smile on the radio announcers faces and hearing the story again, put one right back on my face as well.

CHAPTER 34

One is Such a Lonely Number

Not sure how this topic of conversation got started, especially coming from third graders but this is what I heard. "I'm going to die alone."

"You will not die alone." I responded.

With his eyelids batting profusely and his chin resting on the backside of his laced fingers, he said to me in return, "Not a chance I'm going to die alone...have you seen this face?"

"Yes, Jason. I see your face every day." I told him.

"I know, right?" was his reply. Hmmm. No self-esteem issues with that child!

CHAPTER 35

Just a Little Crush

Whether I am listening to my kids, as we are on our way to school or sitting at the school waiting for the OK to release the kids into the building, I get the opportunity to either talk to them directly or just listen to the children as they are conversing with one another. Most of the time their conversations never fail to amuse or amaze me, much like the following exchange.

One of my third grade boys was telling his seat partner, a second grade boy, about his current girlfriend. This was their exchange.

"I have this very pretty girlfriend. She has long blonde hair and wears dresses a lot. Every day after school, we meet out on the playground for recess, and she kisses my face all over. One time I came home with lipstick covering my whole face." Exclaimed Jason excitedly.

In typical second grade fashion, Alan responded, "Ooh...You have a girlfriend, you have a girlfriend, you have a girlfriend." In that teasing, singsong voice that children use.

Jason most certainly was not going to stand for Alan's taunting, and said, "Well, what can I say; I'm just soooo sweet and at least I like a girl who is my age. You have a crush on some old lady, Mrs. Mileti."

I heard my name, "old and crush," in the same sentence. Thank goodness, we had arrived at the school so I could focus my attention on that conversation.

I turned around to face Jason and said, "Jason, are you telling me that I'm an old lady?"

"No, you're not an old lady," said Jason.

No sooner had Jason told me that I was not an old lady when he turned right back around to his seat partner and said, "You have a crush on an old lady...you have a crush on an old lady." In the same, taunting singsong tone, Alan used just moments before.

Throughout Alan's second and third grade years, he called me "Mrs. My Lady."

CHAPTER 36

Flash Dance

On a dark morning, late in the fall, I was picking up my elementary students. I picked up one of my favorites whom happens to sit directly behind me and shortly after he sat down, Alan asked, "Mrs. My Lady, do you have a flashlight?"

"Yes, I do, Alan."

"May I borrow it?" He asked.

"I can't get it for you right now, Alan, I'm driving. What do you need the flashlight for?" I asked him.

"So I can show everyone on the bus my awesome dance moves!"

Well, what was I thinking? Of course, it was to show off those awesome dance moves. He just needed a spotlight to highlight his efforts. I do not know, but I was thinking that a disco ball would have been a nice add-on to my bus!

What made this even funnier is that the next morning, Alan brought his very own flashlight or should I call it a spotlight to school with him. Yes, he did!

CHAPTER 37

45 Billion Years Ago

I have my second graders sitting up front, my fifth graders in the back, and my third and fourth graders sequentially between them. There is one exception to that rule. The first row of seats is my reserved seating area, for my very special friends. Of which, I have yet to assign, to anyone this year. This, for me, is HUGE (I am laughing as I write this, because an image of Jimmy Kimmel imitating Donald Trump just popped into my brain.) It is the very first time this has occurred in the sixteen years I have been driving. See what I mean...HUGE. (Giggling again).

Alan, one of my all-time favorites, asked me if he could sit up front one afternoon in September. Inwardly, I did a happy dance because once they move back, my opportunities to speak with them, greatly diminishes. I said, "Of course you can sit up front. You can sit behind me and we can talk the whole ride home." His response was, "Yes!" Alan walked back to retrieve his things, bringing them up front.

Upon seeing Alan move to the front row, Larry, a second grader, asked Alan why he was sitting up front. Everyone knows, about my reserved seating section, making Larry jump to the invalid conclusion that Alan was in trouble and was being forced to sit there. Alan told Larry that it was cool to sit up front, so he could talk to me. This prompted Larry to sit up front as well.

Before we left the school lot, I told Alan that it had been a long time since I had seen any of his awesome dance moves. Alan chuckled, but did not say much. I continued with a similar line of questioning, and asked him if he remembered the time he asked me for a flashlight, so he could spotlight his awesome dance moves, on a dark morning ride to school. He said he remembered, and chuckled again. The second grader sitting next to Alan, asked him about the incident.

Alan replied, "Oh that was sooooo long ago. I don't do that anymore. Now, I'm a role model for second graders. Besides that happened like—about 45 billion years ago."

Yes, that was a B for billion. His comment quickly terminated that subject, but not before putting a huge smile on my face or knowing that it had only been about three years since the flashlight incident actually took place.

Alan decided it was his turn to start asking the questions. His first one was a doozy. "Mrs. Mileti, (though he started to call my Mrs. My Lady, his pronunciation of my name since he was in the second grade) which, according to him, was nearly 45 billion years ago, or something like that. "Are you going to retire soon?"

You know that sound you hear on a record (aging myself just a bit) when you slide the needle along the record? That was the sound that echoed in my brain. What? "No," I said. "Does it look like I need to retire?" I asked.

"No," he said.

"Why do you ask?" was my reply.

"Because I want all the second graders to have you as their school bus driver, just like I did."

Gosh, I adore this child was what I was thinking. And once again, I was about brought to tears with his generous compliment.

The next day when Alan got on the bus, he sat down behind me and was clearly still thinking about our retirement conversation. He persisted with his questioning with regards to me retiring.

"When are you going to retire, Mrs. Mileti?" He asked.

"Oh, Alan, don't worry about that. I won't be retiring for a very long time. It will probably be about 12 to 15 years before I retire." I said.

Alan's eyes widened, to roughly the size of saucers when I gave him my answer.

"That will make me..." I could see him doing the math in his head "...about 25. I'll be out of school, married, and have children before you retire."

What could I do, but laugh. The boy has plans and goals for the next fifteen years.

Alan went on to ask me if I knew who the middle school bus driver was for that route. He said he had talked with his friends and they said, "She was kinda nice."

He said, "I didn't know exactly what that means, but guess I'll find out soon enough."

Poor guy, he is already stressing about who his driver is going to be next year and we are not even a full quarter into his fifth grade year.

I assured him that all would be well. That I knew the driver and that she was nice.

For some reason, I felt the need to add that I do drive a high school route and that maybe I would see him again after he got through middle school. Though that scenario may be a possibility, it is highly unlikely that I would have that route at that time.

I am not sure if I told him that for my benefit, or his. He will definitely be one of the ones that I will miss—dearly.

CHAPTER 38

Bieber Fever

Often times, as the bus empties, I have a few students that will move up front to speak with me before they leave for the day. Justin is one of those people.

On this particular day, when Justin moved up, there was a newer song on the radio that all the kids were going nuts over and I was asked to turn up the volume. I obliged their request and turned up the radio. When Justin sat down, I proceeded to ask him if the person singing was Justin Bieber. Justin confirmed that indeed, it was Bieber. As he was responding, Justin rolled his eyes and gave an audible sigh of disgust.

"Not a fan I take it?" I said.

"I guess he's all right. I mean most of the time it's OK that we share the same name. Which is all right, I guess. But he gets all the girls and can buy anything he wants." He replied.

"Now Justin," I asked, "what on earth would you do with all those girls? Girls are nothing but trouble!"

To which he replied, "Good point...wait a second, Mrs. Mileti, you're a girl that means your trouble too."

"You're absolutely right, Justin, but I'm trouble with a capital T."

He repeated what I said as if he was trying it out to see how it sounded or if it fit then, I was rewarded with a hearty laugh and complete agreement that I was, in fact, trouble with a capital T.

CHAPTER 39

I Have a Question

I have a number of students who enjoy coming to the front of the bus to chat with me when we are parked at the school waiting for the school doors to be open and released from the school bus. I have two fourth grade girls in particular who come forward and regularly ask me trivia questions. On this particular day, Rene came forward and said, "We have another question to ask you Mrs. Barrometti."

Mrs. Barrometti? "What's my name, Rene?" I asked.

"Oh, whoops, sorry, that's my teacher's name, and I sometimes get them confused. You know, Barrometti Mileti they both end in etti. Anyway, what are the two largest ____" (I could not understand the word she was using) "regions in Ohio?" She asked.

To which I responded, "Could you repeat the question please?" Which, she did. I still did not understand the word she was using before the word region.

"I'm sorry Rene; I'm just not quite sure what your question is. Are you asking which regions or cities are most densely populated? Or are you asking, which regions have the largest land mass? I'm just not quite sure what you are asking." I replied.

At this point, she put one hand on her hip and with her other hand, started wagging her finger at me. A finger wag! "Now Mrs. Mileti (funny, she got my name right that time) this is a fourth grade social studies question. You should know the answer," she said.

"I'm sorry Rene; I still don't understand the question."

She gave me very loud audible disgusted sigh and said, "Let me give you an easier word, region. Do you understand the word region?"

Okay, really? What I am thinking is—you are really cruising for a bruising little girl! However, I replied, "Yes, I understand the word region. I'm still just not sure what you are referring to."

"Oh, never mind, we have an easier question for you. Do male penguins take care of the egg on their feet?" To which I replied (relieved that I actually knew the answer.) "Empire male penguins set the egg on their feet covering it with their belly feathers until it hatches. But, not all penguins do that."

"Exactly right! I knew you would get that one right, that was an easy one."

Gee, thanks kid! You USED to be one of my all-time favorites.

Clearly, I should never be a contestant on *Are You Smarter than a Fifth Grader*! Cuz, I is not. Apparently, I do not even measure up to that of a fourth grade level.

After all of my students departed, I quickly pulled out my smartphone to find the answer. I Googled two largest regions of Ohio. Lo and behold, what she was trying to ask was; "What are the two largest physio geographic regions in Ohio." Well, let me tell you something, kid. First, I am from Minnesota. Second, I have not had fourth grade social studies in over 40 years. Third, really—who cares? Just in case you are dying to know the answer, and for those of you who are also challenged by this very easy fourth grade social studies question, the answers are in order of size biggest to smallest: (1) Till plains (Central Lowland), (2) Unglaciated Appalachian Plateaus (Allegheny Plateaus), (3) Glaciated Allegheny Plateaus, (4) Lake

Plains, (5) Bluegrass. You were just about to guess that, weren't you? Whew, aren't you glad you know? Well, I know I can die a very happy girl finally knowing this information. Shoot, I cannot believe I lived as long as I did without this knowledge.

CHAPTER 40

Unforgettable

Sometimes, a child comes along and makes such an impact on your life that when they leave, it leaves a giant empty hole in your heart. Such was the case when little Miss Maria walked through my bus doors. Maria is in foster care. She proclaimed this fact the first day I met her. Maria was an adorable second grader with a toothless grin that made the whole bus alight with her cheerfulness and the sparkle in her eyes added to the warmth this child emitted.

I knew Maria struggled with reading, but she never seemed discouraged by this and forged on as best she could. One day in October, Maria walked on the bus and handed me a handmade card. I am always thrilled when I receive something from a child. I am especially excited when it is something that a child took the time to draw, write, or make with me in mind. I accepted the note and thanked her for it. When we arrived at school, however, she asked if I would open and read the card. So, I did.

My smile quickly faded as I read the card. It said, "I'm going to miss you so much! I will remember riding bus 20 every day. I will not be riding bus 20 anymore."

I asked Maria what was going on and why she would not be riding my bus any longer. She responded that she was moving. I said, "Oh, you and your family are moving?"

She replied, "No, my sister and I are getting a new foster mom and a new school, and Thursday is my last day."

It felt as if all the air had been sucked off the bus and my lungs were incapable of functioning. I struggled desperately to hold back my tears and to try to spin the situation in a positive light. I told her what an exciting time this was for her and her sister, and what a grand adventure she and her sister were certain to have. I prayed that change would be positive and joyful. Inwardly hating that I could not wrap her in my arms, tell her everything was going to be OK, and simply bring her home with me. Moments after the children left for the morning, the tears fell. Then again, that happens every time I recall this story.

Now, I still had my middle school route to complete. Being emotionally upset and completely distracted while you are at work sitting behind your desk, is one-thing. It is entirely another, when your office is a 40 foot long, 13 ton vehicle packed with other people's children who rely and expect you to be focused and composed at all times to keep their children safe. The point I am trying to make here is that it took a herculean effort to make it through my final route of the morning that day. Blessedly, the morning crawled to an end. I returned home knowing that I wanted to get something for Maria. I bought her something that I hoped would be a lasting, joyful keepsake. I bought her a toy school bus and personalized it with the number 20 in all the right places, accompanied with a card. That afternoon, I gave her the gift, which I put in a pretty pink and green gift bag. She was thrilled to get the gift and asked if she could open it on the bus. I told her that would be fine, and she did. I was rewarded with the most beatific toothless grin. She opened the card, looked at it, giving me yet another fabulous smile. Then, she asked if I could read it to her. I said of course, I would read it to her. It said, "Here's a hug, just for you, just because...." I also wrote that I would miss her too, to stay sweet, and to keep making life sparkle! At this moment, I was really struggling with the whole foster care program. Of course, I was not privy to the whys of what was happening. Nevertheless, as an outsider looking in, this was again, breaking my heart. Uprooting Maria and her sister from the only foster parents, they had known, to another home, a completely different city, and a totally different school district. How could any of this be beneficial, for not only her emotional well-being, but her educational growth as well? How much more would this push back any progress she could hope to make to eliminate her reading and writing difficulties?

The next day, Maria got on the bus and she had the gift bag in tow, she wanted to show her teacher what I had given her. Now, it was my turn to smile! Maria's parting gift to me was a big hug and one last amazing smile as she left the bus for the last time. Once again, I found myself fighting back the tears.

A few days later, while picking up my elementary students in the afternoon, one of the staff members of the school approached me, told me which school district she had been placed in and assured me it was a very good school district. Her reassuring words did help me feel better about Maria and her situation, though I will always wonder what ever happened to my sweet little toothless Maria. It is rare that I ever learn what becomes of the students that I transport once they move on. For the children who have younger siblings, I will occasionally get some updates from them, or may see them in the future on a field trip, usually, I have them for three to five years, and then, they just move on. Some students, however, will remain with me forever!

CHAPTER 41

Hocus Pocus

Halloween can prove to be fun, interesting, and challenging, all rolled into one, for a school bus driver. Most districts will allow you to wear a costume, as long as you do not have anything obstructing your vision. Over the years, I have been Red Riding Hood, a witch (numerous years), Velma from Scooby Doo, a cat, and most recently, an angel.

Every year in October, at some point, the children start discussing costumes. I always ask what the children are going to dress up as and they eagerly share their ideas with me. Occasionally, a few of my kids will ask me in return, what or whom I am thinking of dressing up as. This particular year, three of my second graders were interested in what my costume would be. I said that I had not yet decided and I would have to give it some thought.

A few days later, Abby, one of my second graders, approached me and asked if I had decided what I was going to be for Halloween. The truth was I had not given it a second thought since the conversation was brought up the first time. I told Abby that I still had not yet decided, but I was sure I would choose soon.

The next day, I was asked the same question from Abby. This time, since I still had not thought much about it, I told her it is a secret and you will find out on Halloween. Ha! I did not even know myself! The next day, Abby got on the bus and she said, "Why won't you tell me what you are going to be for Halloween?"

I told her it would not be much of a secret if I told her. She assured me that if I did tell her that she would keep my secret and not share it with any of the other children. How cute is that? The truth of the matter was I did not know myself, and so, it was a secret, even to me.

I had contemplated not dressing up that year, but after telling Abby that my costume was a secret, I knew that was no longer an option. So, I set about looking for a costume. Something simple, that would not require a great deal of effort.

Finally, I decided what I was going to be for Halloween. True to my word though, I kept my costume identity to myself and made my young friends wait to see what I had chosen.

Halloween arrived. I put on my wings and halo with a gleaming white turtleneck and some glow sticks for affect.

My high school kids are the first to be picked up in the morning and since they are still primarily asleep, I do not think any of them actually noticed.

Next are my elementary students. My little second grade, Abby, was sure to be curious as to what my appearance would be like. I got to her stop midway through the route and when she entered the bus, I expected an immediate reaction. Abby sat in the first row. To my surprise, Abby did not immediately comment when she boarded the bus. Shortly after she sat down, however, she did.

"Mrs. Mileti, you're an angel, but it doesn't look like you are wearing a costume."

"What do you mean Abby? I have on wings and a halo." In my mind, I am thinking how is it possible you cannot see the halo and wings. They are not a typical part of my everyday apparel.

Then, she said, "You are an angel every day."

Her comment almost made me cry! I think it is probably one of the nicest comments anyone has ever told me.

I returned to the bus garage later that morning, beaming. Abby made my day with her sweet comment. When I arrived, my supervisor, George, was there, waiting to speak with all the drivers returning from their morning runs. I approached George and I was advised that costumes would not be permitted during the afternoon routes. This would apply for both drivers and aides. This, as I am walking in with my wings and halo on. I immediately took them off and asked him what was going on.

One of our drivers wore a costume that scared a child, prompting a parent, a teacher, and an administrator to call in and complain. This brought my angel impersonation to an abrupt finish.

The afternoon quickly turned into a freakish rendition of *A Nightmare on Elm Street*, only in this instance, the nightmare was a daymare, and my nightmare occurred on Waterbury Woods Dr. Three quarters of the way through my high school route, while turning west on Waterbury Woods Drive, I turned down a street that was lined with cars, on both sides of the road. Typically, this is not a problem, and I can easily maneuver my bus through most obstacle courses I encounter on any given day and quite readily, I might add. There was, however, one minor, OK, major problem. This particular street was lined with cars on both sides. There was certainly not room enough for two vehicles traveling in opposite directions to make it through. As it was, I had about a foot on either side of my bus with a solid line of vehicles lined up on

146

both sides, all the way to the stop signs and almost into the intersecting street, with a vehicle to the rear, making it impossible for me to move in any direction. So, there I sat, waiting for the vehicles heading toward me to turn around and go the other way. Two vehicles did exactly that, but one would get turned around, and another would turn down the road I was trying to leave. I radioed for assistance saying that it was likely that we would need the police to help remedy this situation.

The situation went from bad to worse, as a day care van turned down the road blocking the two cars trying to get turned around. One of the cars was somewhat sandwiched between myself and the daycare van, the driver of the car, a woman, in her mid to late 30's got out of her vehicle and sauntered over to my bus. She approached my window and asked if I was stuck. Wow! Keen observation Captain Obvious, was what I was thinking. "Yes. There's not much I can do." All the while thinking to myself, no, I am sitting here watching the show. What do you think?—Keeping those thoughts to myself. What came out of her mouth next absolutely blew my mind away! She said, "So, you're going to inconvenience all of these people who have a function to attend because you can't move your bus?"

If you have not guessed it by now, I took great offense to her comment and replied out the window, "Would you like to do this job?"

To which she promptly replied, "No, I don't. Why are you being so rude? I'm just trying to figure out what's going on here. That's why I came over here."

Really? I thought, you could not figure that out simply by looking at scenario playing out before us. I am in a 40-foot long vehicle, with vehicles on both sides of the road, and vehicles coming in my direction. I cannot make a left hand turn without my tail swing taking out one of the parked cars on the right and I cannot back up with all the vehicles behind me as well. But, I am the one being rude? You just insulted me, but I am the one being rude? WOW! I was actually very glad I was not wearing the angel costume now. My blood was boiling! Making matters worse, it was twenty minutes into this ordeal. I had already done a whole lot of me "inconveniencing" the parents of the daycare facility. Even though it was they, who failed to provide the necessary accommodations for all the parents visiting that day or the security to maintain a decent traffic flow. There was still no assistance from the local sheriff's department, though finally, a daycare worker came out and attempted to bring some order to the chaos that was happening all around me.

Meanwhile, the natives inside the bus were getting restless. I still had kids onboard wondering when we were going to make it out of that mess. Even the remaining students on my bus could see why we were not going anywhere and found the accusations of the belligerent parent ridiculous. The daymare finally ended, twenty-five minutes after it began. I was finally able to maneuver my way out of that plat, with the assistance of one of the daycare workers. Once I completed my high school route, my boss blessedly covered my remaining middle school route, so my daymare was finally ending, saving me from the boiling rage that was building up in me with each passing moment. I think I could actually feel the devil horns sprouting, instantly transforming the place where my halo sat just hours earlier into a ghoulish whacked-out maniac. Now, not only was my angel moment short lived, it now just seemed like a distant dream.

CHAPTER 42

Reserved Seating

Every now and again, I get to witness something wonderful about some of the kids I am transporting. Usually, this happens entirely by accident. On this particular afternoon, one of my students, Kevin, had a very difficult time remaining in his seat. After I had verbally asked him to sit down and remain seated, for the third time, I made Kevin move up to the front of the bus in one of my reserved seating areas. A dreadful punishment for a fifth grade boy! For in doing so, Kevin would be made to sit next to a second grader—gasp! Worse yet, his only option, at the time were all second grade girls. Trust me; in the eyes of a fifth grade boy, it does not get much worse than that.

Kevin begrudgingly plopped himself down next to Jane and sat as far away as the bus seat would allow, while still remaining in the seat. Jane, on the other hand was thrilled to have the company and proceeded to chatter up a storm with Kevin. At the time, I did not give the interaction between the two much thought nor did I pay that much attention to it. She was engaging him in conversation and he was tolerating and enduring his punishment. The remainder of the ride home was an easy one.

When I move a child from the back of the bus to the front of the bus, it is rarely for just that ride home. It is kind of like being grounded and the duration of the punishment largely depends on what type of behavior I am trying to modify. So, the following morning, Kevin got on the bus and did not even ask where he should sit, he just sat down in the same seat as the afternoon before. Once again, Jane was thrilled to have her seat partner returning that next morning. That afternoon, Kevin asked if he could sit in the back, and in return I asked if he would be able to remain seated, to which he promised he would. So, I sent him on his way and he was quite pleased to return to his fifth grade friends! Jane on the other hand was not as thrilled with my decision to let Kevin go back to his assigned seat.

The next morning, when Kevin got on the bus, and made his back to his assigned seat, Jane looked up as Kevin was passing her and asked, "Kevin, will you sit with me?"

I was expecting Kevin to acknowledge her request and politely decline her offer, or for him to ignore Jane altogether and continue to his seat without a hint of acknowledgment of her request. To my utter shock and disbelief and without doubt or hesitation, Kevin sat down next to Jane. He was not only patient and kind, but also attentive and compassionate. Some days Kevin would get on the bus, Jane would ask him to sit by her and Kevin would say, "I'm going to sit in back today, but I'll sit with you tomorrow." True to his word, he did. This little ritual continued off and on until Emily, a new student, became Jane's new seat partner. Well done Mr. & Mrs. Adams, very well done indeed! What a fine young man you are raising! As Kevin's school bus driver, my heart was bursting with pride, so, Mr. and Mrs. Adams, you have much to be proud of!

CHAPTER 43

Dirty Dancing

The other day, while dropping off one of my students, I glanced into my student mirror and saw what appeared to be one of my other students, twerking in the aisle, towards the back of the bus. I picked up the mic to the intercom on my bus and told this child, "This is a twerk free zone."

He promptly responds, "I'm not twerking, I'm pooping."

"You're what?" Gasp! Now guess whom has the shocked look on their face? Yep, that'd be me! Thankfully, one of the other children in back, clarified, that he was imitating a dog that they had viewed, doing his business just minutes before. Whew! Because if he was pooping, my next comment would have been—on second thought— twerk zone—definitely, a twerk zone. Twerk on!

That is what I get for trying to be funny! For those of you who may not know what twerking is, I

153

give you this explanation. It is this generation's version of dirty dancing. If you need a further visual reference, YouTube it.

CHAPTER 44

Sassy Pants

Squabbles and minor disagreements break out on my school bus on a regular basis. Typically, ending in one of the children coming forward to tattle on whatever infraction or injustice they believe has taken place. Such was the case for this next story.

Adam, my resident tattletale, marched up to inform me that his brother, Melvin told him that Sheridan came up to him with her fist like this (his small fist raised up facing me) and gave him the middle finger, which, of course, he felt necessary to demonstrate.

"Did you see it happen?" I asked.

"No" replied Adam.

"Well, then that may not have been what happened, if you did not see it." I responded.

Now, Ellen, a second grader sitting behind me, pipes in and says, "I think Sheridan did that."

"Why do you think Sheridan did that, Ellen?" I asked.

Ellen, (with her hands on her hips) "Because, Sheridan told me that she was born sassy and there is nothing she can do about it."

Buwhahahaha! Why did not I think of that excuse? That has become my new mantra—and there is nothing you can do about it. ☺

CHAPTER 45

Check...1...2...Check

You know it is loud when you can no longer block out the noise emanating from behind you. Blocking out noise, by the way, is a hallmark skill that most school bus drivers have mastered, mainly to retain their sanity, if there was ever any sanity there to begin with. Anyway, they were LOUD!

In my attempt to reign them in, I picked up my internal intercom and attempted to ask them to dial it back a few dozen decibels. I pushed the transmission button and started speaking and—nothing. I did what most people would do to remedy the problem—I hit it. Then, I tried again, but was met with the same result—nothing. Meanwhile, one of my students, a favorite of mine, was watching and listening to what I was trying to do. When the mic did not transmit the first time, he watched me smack the thing in my hand and try again. When it would not work the second time, he wondered out loud, as to why the mic was not functioning and offered up his hypothesis. He had done so, with his head tilted to one side, and a perplexed look on his face. "Do you think it's not working because you use it so much?"

To which I replied, "Ya know Alan, you might be right."

Then, he proceeded to ask me how much the mic cost and where he could get one, cause he could really use one of those!

Take a number, kid. I need one too! Turned out to be a loose cord connection, NOT,—cough, cough, over use, as originally suggested.

CHAPTER 46

Fun Start to My Day

The door entering into my bus was stuck; I could not open it by myself, so I asked for assistance from one of the mechanics. So, what does he bring to open it? A blowtorch, because that is the first thing one thinks of to open a door that is stuck. NOT. Anyway, Dave was convinced that I locked the door even though the keys were dangling from the ignition. The blowtorch was not working, so I decided to try get in through the rear door to see if I could push it open from the inside.

I am not sure when or if you have ever attempted to climb into the back of a school bus, but lemme tell ya...the words grace and elegance would never have been used to describe my efforts! Let us just say being short was not beneficial in this instance. Not to mention, the outcome was fruitless! I did manage to hoist myself up into the back of the bus and pushed on the door as Dave was pulling, but the door remained stuck. Dave was still convinced I locked the door—somehow. So I handed him the keys through the window and he tried the key with no success—shocker.

So, back to the blowtorch, which, when applied to the top portion of the door starts smoking. Umm hello, I am still on the bus. Then, like magic, the sucker opened.

I returned midway through my route to use the facilities, got off bus, shut the door, again, and left the keys in the ignition with engine running, when I came out, the damn thing locked up again. This time Dave's tool of choice was a hammer. Worked like a charm. Guess all it really needed was a little hammer time. Thanks, Dave!

CHAPTER 47

Nothing to Talk About

One of my fourth grade boys was boarding the bus; I noticed that he had a blue Post-It note taped to the front of his shirt. I could not read what it said, but I could see that the writing on the note was written in pencil and that a youthful hand had written it. I presume it was his writing. I was curious as to what the note said, so I asked him if I could read his note. He came back to the front of the bus and faced me, revealing the note taped to his shirt.

This is what it said:

"WON'T talk till next week...unless important." The last part was written in much smaller letters.

I could not resist, I just had to test out his delightful little proclamation, and so I asked him why he was not going to talk until next week. He raised his eyebrows and dramatically directed his

161

hands toward the note attached to his chest, then quickly went back to his seat.

Well, his silence lasted, at best, five minutes. I had Christmas music playing. When *Rudolph the Red Nosed Reindeer* started playing, it promptly ended his vow of silence for the week. Then again, he was not exactly talking, and singing about Rudolph might just classify as being important.

CHAPTER 48

Once Bitten

"Hey, Mrs. Mileti, guess what happened to me this weekend?" Adam asked.

"I have no idea, Adam. What happened?

"I got bit by a snake—TWICE!" He told me.

"Oh my goodness, how awful! Where did that happen?" I asked.

"In my yard."

"Ask him how he got bit by the snake." His brother shouted, as Adam was telling his story.

"How did you get bit by the snake, Adam?" I asked.

"I picked him up by the tail and spun him around, like this." Adam proceeded to give me a visual reenactment of his encounter with the snake. He swung his arm around in a rather wild lasso-type motion indicating a very wild ride for the snake, which, resulted in the snake ultimately biting his finger at some point.

"How did it happen the second time?" I asked.

"I did it again." He said.

"And you were surprised by the snakes response the second time around?"

Well, I think he can eliminate snake charmer as a possible career choice.

CHAPTER 49

Can I Have This Dance?

In the morning before I can release my elementary students from the bus, we must wait until a representative from the school gives us a signal that they are ready to receive them. Even after we get the thumbs up, we are limited as to the number of busses that can be released at one time. What this means is that I sit with my students for approximately eight minutes before they get their green light to go.

While we wait, the radio is on, and the volume goes up when a favorite song is playing, as was the case on that day. One of my third graders who sits towards the back was in the aisle facing the students that sit behind him. At that moment, the music moved him to shake his booty in grand style. He proceeded to entertain the kids siting behind him, and unbeknown to him, me. That was, at least, until he spun around and realized that I was watching his mad skills on his makeshift dance floor.

Apparently, showing off to one's peers is far more desirable than having—gasp—an adult, worse yet, your school bus driver witness this awesome spectacle—NO—not that, anything but that! He quickly turned an impressive shade of red that even outmatched the beautiful red that naturally adorns his head. The only thing more remarkable...save the dance moves...was his ability to return to his seat with a speed, that Mercury himself would have marveled.

CHAPTER 50

Joy to the World?

Approximately 11 years ago, my child and a host of other children, from the bus, taught me a modified version of *Joy to the World*, with alternate lyrics, and a host of other delightful songs. When we moved south, I expected to hear many of these same tunes, which tend to be passed on primarily for their silly factor. I was somewhat surprised when I arrived expecting to hear those little ditties, but alas, they did not make their way to my ears.

The familiar tune and those unmistakable lyrics eventually made a comeback. However, I did have to make a few minor lyrical corrections, which were an instant hit. After which, I was treated to a very lively and raucous presentation that lasted the duration of our ride home.

For those of you who are unfamiliar with the altered version of this song, I will provide you with the alternate lyrics so you too can experience the joy. The character in the song being referenced can be either Barney, as in Barney the dinosaur, or Barbie...sung, of course, to the tune of *Joy to the World.*

> "Joy to the World, Barney's dead,
> we barbequed his head. Don't worry
> about the body...we flushed it down
> the potty...around and around it goes...."

What ever happened to *The Wheels on the Bus Go Round and Round*?

Welcome to my world!

CHAPTER 51

Remote Control

I have a very loud third grade boy on my bus. On this day, I just could not tune out his piercingly loud, unmistakably distinctive tone, which radiates above any other child's voice onboard. I asked him if he had volume control, or, better yet, a mute button. He shook his head no. One of my third grade girls stuck out her hand offering up her makeshift mute button and told me to push it. I pushed it—did not work, darn it! As one of my second graders was going to get off the bus, she handed me a piece of paper with a circle drawn on it with the word mute written in the middle of the circle. She handed it to me and said, "Here, Mrs. Mileti, it's Adam's mute button."

Apparently, I was not the only one who thought Adam needed a mute button.

CHAPTER 52

Gotta Go

Sometimes, it is difficult being the last stop on a route, particularly when you have to go to the bathroom and there is not a bathroom in sight.

"We gotta move this process along Mrs. Mileti, I gotta take a dump." Joe proclaimed as he was walking up the aisle toward me.

"Joe, I will get you home as fast and legally as I possibly can." I replied.

"No you're not, you're going 15 m.p.h." He sneered.

"I'm doing the speed limit, Joe." I told him.

"The speed limit is 25 M.P.H. and you're driving 15 m.p.h."

"Joe, you're reading my tachometer." I said

"What's a tachometer?"

"It measures the speed of the engine."

"Oh, I didn't know that," said Joe.

Thankfully, we arrived at his stop.

"We're here, Joe. How'd I do?" I asked him.

"Not bad, Mrs. Mileti, not bad at all."

Distraction and keeping him talking—huh, it worked!

Whew! Dodged a bullet, on that one.

Chapter 53

Not Quite Ready

Fourth grade wisdom:

"My birthday is coming up soon." Joe told me.

"Great! How old are you going to be? Ten?" I asked.

"Well, technically, I'm going to be 11."

"What do you mean 'technically'?" I asked.

"Well, you know the 14-months you spend in your mom's tummy." He told me.

"It's actually a little less than a year, closer to nine months." I said.

"No, no, I'm pretty sure it was 14-months I was in there; and even when I did come out, I wasn't ready to come out." He told me.

"So, did they put you back in there?" I asked him.

I couldn't help it, my sarcastic remark just slipped out.

I know, I know! Bad, bad, bus driver! Sorry guys, I just could not help myself. ☺

CHAPTER 54

Karate Kid

One of my fourth grade boys was standing at the bottom of the stairs, in his best "Karate Kid" pose. His head was adorned with a narrow, white, and black headband tied around his head. He was wearing an all-black sweat suit. "I'm a najinja. A ninja and a ginja." He told me.

I must have had a puzzled look on my face, since after which, he proceeded to break it down and said, "Ninja" his hands sweeping up and down the black tracksuit that he is wearing. Then, he says "ginja" and his hands swirl around the top of his head indicating his hair, which is a lovely shade of red or ginger, a slang term for red heads. "Najinja!" he proclaimed.

CHAPTER 55

Looking Good

"Mrs. Mileti, would you like to see my new glasses?" Elizabeth, a third grader, asked me.

"I'd love to see your new glasses, Elizabeth." I told her. "Ooh! They look lovely...and they're your favorite color too! Pink." I added.

"I can see her getting smarter by the minute," said Molly, Elizabeth's seat partner, once Elizabeth placed the glasses on her face.

I am still trying to decide if, Molly was being punny, or, if she was being sweet to her friend.

I could see it going either way, then again, hindsight's 20/20.

CHAPTER 56

Only the Lonely

One of my sixth graders and I were having a conversation one afternoon. He was telling me all about his weekend. While we were speaking, one if his siblings asked to whom he was speaking. "I'm speaking with the bus driver." He said.

To which she responds, "You must be R E A L L Y lonely."

I just loved her strong emphasis on "really," and the puzzled, bordering on disgusted tone to her statement. Yikes! What am I—chopped liver? ☺

CHAPTER 57

Kidisms

<u>Kidism 1</u>

"I had the worst day of my whole life yesterday," said Terri, a second grade girl.

"What happened to make it the worst day of your life?" I asked her. "I had a test and I had to study for it," she replied.

I did not have the heart to tell her there will be a host of "worst days ever" ahead of her, if that is the criteria for worst days.

<u>Kidism 2</u>

Observation of Joe, a fifth grade boy.

"The bus looks like it's taking a selfie. Look in those mirrors up there."

He was pointing to the convex mirrors on the front of the bus and looking at the mirror reflection of the bus in the mirror.

Kidism 3

Third graders take on Santa.

Santa has been around for like...4,000 years. I think he was born in the 60's.

Talk about speeding up the aging process!

Kidism 4

I drove a new bus this morning, which for my elementary kids was a really big deal.

"The seats are blue."

"This bus smells bad."

"This bus is weird."

These were just a few of the comments I heard, then, one of my second graders comes to this conclusion...

"It's because it's a high school bus."

Kidism 5

The elementary kids are getting off the bus this morning.

Lenny: Mrs. Mileti, Maura hit a kid.

Me: Maura, did you hit someone?

Maura: Ya can't blame me.

Me: Whom did you hit?

Maura: I don't know his name, he's just an annoying little second grader, and he was all up in my space.

Well that is some serious rationalization and justification for you!

Kidism 6

"The sky is filled with cotton candy."

One of my third graders describing the gorgeous "cotton candy" colored sky and clouds one morning. I just love how they view the world around them.

Kidism 7

Second grade boy, "I know why my throat hurts so much. I'm getting my big man voice...yes!"

Hmm, think that might have another name— like strep throat?

Kidism 8

Elana: Mrs. Mileti, is it true that if you look in the mirror and say Bloody Mary three times, something bad will happen?

Me: No, it's not true.

Monica: Oh, she doesn't know, she's too old. Look it up on the internet. It's true!

Kidism 9

One morning when it was particularly icy out and while I was unloading my elementary kids. One of my fifth grade boys was exiting the bus; he hit a patch of ice, just past the bus doors on the right-hand side. He recovered the near fall after an impressive wobble, but instead on continuing into the school, he walked back in front of my door, with a grand smile lighting up his face, looking quite pleased with himself, and says, "I landed it."

Kidism 10

"That blonde back there seriously needs to download a new app for her attitude."

It always amazes me that they do not know one another's names.

Kidism 11

As one of my fifth graders was getting off the bus, he approached me and proceeded to give me an awkward hug, after which, he made a very hasty exit from the bus. The next day, as he was getting off the bus, he walked by without giving me a hug. Teasingly, I said "What? No hug today?" He was standing on the bus steps when I asked him the question. He turned, looked at me, and said, "It was a dare."

I was caught off guard by his response and, frankly, somewhat speechless, amused, but definitely at a loss for words. Since that day, and every day, thereafter, until he moved on to middle school, whenever he got off the bus, he patted me on the head.

A dare... I have to say, that was a first. Think I preferred the awkward hug.

Kidism 12

One of my high school students got on the bus and told me that his birthday was the next day. I proceeded to ask him how he was planning to celebrate his birthday. He shared with me his plans. I then asked him if he was going to be 16. He replied no, that he would be 17. That is kind of unusual. Usually, once they get their license, they cannot get off the bus fast enough. Anyway, I said well, we have something in common; my birthday is in April too. He asked me when, and I told him. Then, I said, "Only I'm a couple years older than you, like one or two, decades...," OK, so it is three, but I was not putting that out there.

To which he replied, "So, will you be 28?"

Well hello, new best friend, and favorite rider! I knew I liked that kid! ☺

Kidism 13

One of my second graders was lamenting to the students seated around her about what a horrible, mean school bus driver I am. Her less than flattering comments were repeated by, none other than, my resident tattletale and his seat partner. I am not too sure if I was annoyed or flattered by their rendition of what had been said...regardless, I told my second grader that while she was definitely entitled to her opinion, that if she did not have nice things to say, that she should consider keeping those comments to herself. Ha! As if! I should heed my own advice. Far too often, I will think something, and then blurt out the thought I was just thinking, after which, I think to myself—was that out loud? Anyway....

Now, we fast-forward a few weeks. As we were approaching my biggest fan's stop and as she was preparing to leave, she proclaimed to me "Best bus ride home ever!" and she handed me a note card that said she loved me.

About time, she realized how amazing I am. Ha-ha!

Kidism 14

"You never want to be a first grader! They never get to have recess, or go outside, or do anything. They sit in the corner and do nothing all day. Then, they get on the bus and teach the fifth graders how to cuss."

I would cuss too, if I had to sit in the corner all day doing nothing.

Kidism 15

"I just can't get over how different you look when you're not sitting in that seat," said Bradley, one of my sixth grade boys.

"What's different about how I look?" I asked him.

"Well, you look thinner, you look younger, and you look shorter." He told me.

Now, if I could just figure out a way to drive the bus while standing.

Kidism 16

Jon: I'm Irish and German.

Sam: I'm mainly English and German, but I'm a little Korean.

Conor: My cousin says I'm one centimeter Japanese.

Jon: Conor, you can't measure nationality with a metric ruler.

Conor is blond with blue eyes. His one centimeter must be hiding. ☺

CHAPTER 58

My Children

It is quite likely that my children have no idea the positive impact they have had on my life. The smiles, laughter, and joy they have brought into my life are endless, and the gratitude I feel for all of them is at times, overwhelming. The children are the spring in my step, the sparkle in my eyes, and the very reason I choose to remain a school bus driver. I cannot imagine doing anything else that could provide me the level of happiness this job brings into my life. That is not to say there has not been some challenging moments throughout my driving career, but the good far outweighs the negative and my joy is overflowing!

About the Author

Therese was born and raised in a suburb of Minneapolis, MN. She is one of four children and boasts being the only girl, making her, her father's all-time favorite daughter. Her youngest brother, Tim, has Down syndrome, so she came to have an appreciation and compassion for all levels of capabilities in people. She spent her school years as most children do, engaged in school and extra circular activities. Which for her, included soccer and singing; though not done at the same time. Therese graduated from high school and attended Bemidji State University.

Therese started her school bus driving career in Aurora, Ohio and has been driving for sixteen years. The past ten of which, have been spent with the Centerville City School District, located in Centerville, Ohio (a suburb of Dayton). Therese is a certified On Board Instructor and has had the pleasure of training over one hundred drivers. Therese loves what she does and enjoys her involvement with her children, immensely. Her husband and friends encouraged her to start writing down her daily experiences, so you too can enjoy the colorful antics her children have treated her to over the years.

Though Therese is no longer playing soccer, she continues to sing, both on and off the school bus. When she's not driving her bus or training other drivers, you can find Therese spending time with family and friends.

Acknowledgements

There are a host of people I need to acknowledge that have been instrumental throughout my first book writing endeavor. First and foremost, I need to thank my husband, Nick, our son Dominic, stepson, Anthony, my parents, Don and Kathy, and my brothers, John, Mike, and Tim for their constant encouragement, unwavering support, and unconditional love. To Mark and Jodi who planted the writing seed, inspiring me to start this project, and provided the confidence I needed to make this idea become a reality. Thanks to Patti for assisting me through this writing process and introducing me to my editor and publisher. I need to thank the district I drive for, including the amazing staff and administrators. The atmosphere, and positive working environment make it a pleasure for me to come to work on a daily basis. The people I work with are truly the icing on the cake and I am convinced I could not find a nicer group of people to work with. My family and friends not mentioned above, your contagious optimism gave me the incentive I needed to see this project through to fruition. Last but certainly not least, to my editor/publisher, Laurel. Without her, I could not have made this all come together. I am grateful and blessed for the impact each one of you have had on not only this project, but how each of you have positively influenced my life, in both big and small ways. I am deeply humbled by the kindness each of you has bestowed upon me. For all of that and so much more—I thank you.

THERESE MILETI